THE GRANDEST LOVE

THE GRANDEST LOVE

Inspiring the Grandparent-Grandchild Connection

JERRY WITKOVSKY

Edited by
Vivien Orbach-Smith

To order additional copies of this book, contact:
Xlibris LLC
1-888-795-4274
www.Xlibris.com
Orders@Xlibris.com
113258

"If you look deeply into the palm of your hand, you will see your parents and all generations of your ancestors. All of them are alive in this moment. Each is present in your body. You are the continuation of each of these people."
~THICH NHAT HANH (Vietnamese Zen-Buddhist Monk)

I dedicate this book to the memory of my wife, Margaret, my partner for 52 years; to my daughter, Ellen, and her husband, Don; to my son, Michael, and his wife, Julie; and to the six young people for whom I have "The Grandest Love": my grandchildren—Aidan, Merete, Benny, Kathryn, Ethan, and Jessica.

CONTENTS

Foreword by Joan Maltese, Ph.D. 11

Introduction:
    The Grandest Love: A Love Worth
    "Teaching-And-Learning" About 15
1. My Story:
    An Ongoing Journey toward Grand Connection 31
2. Identifying Your Family's Core Values:
    Workbook for a Grand New Vision.....................................53
3. Gateway to the Grandest Love:
    Rebuilding Trust, Achieving Forgiveness............................77
4. TLC ("Tender Loving Communication"):
    The Grandest Way to Avoid and Resolve Conflict 97
5. The Grand Balance:
    Declaring Our Interdependence...117
6. The World's Our Kitchen Table:
    Grand Ways to Stay Connected...139
7. Making Grand Memories:
    Teaching and Learning, Living and Loving 155
8. A Grand Expedition:
    Creating A Living Legacy..175
9. The Grandchildren Speak
    (Witkovsky Edition)..193
10. All-of-a-Kind Grandkids:
    Resources for Understanding and Hope 205

Grand Thoughts 225

Acknowledgments...229

"The Grandchildren Speak" Index of Contributors....................233

About the Author...235

FOREWORD

As a family psychologist, I was struck by the fact there is often a key factor missing in society's conversations about what makes individuals and families, and especially children, thrive: *our deep need for intergenerational love and support—even in a determinedly self-reliant culture and digital age.*

Grandparents matter. Jerry Witkovsky gets this, and as a new grandparent myself, I find his passion and enthusiasm delightfully contagious, and I plan to heed his call to action. In *The Grandest Love,* he offers practical and creative suggestions for developing meaningful, intentional family traditions that can be adapted to fit any family's circumstances; they will enhance the well-being of all three generations and may be passed on for generations to come.

Jerry's professional wisdom was born of his many years as the esteemed head of a massive Chicago community-center system and as a beloved camp director. And then there's also his personal journey as a grandfather. No family is "perfect," and Jerry is the first to say neither is his. But most families can be better, stronger, and happier. By candidly sharing his journey, Jerry makes us all feel like we can do better too. His sage advice comes from transformative experiences that offer hope for real growth in family relationships—change that may appear small but is in fact deep and lasting.

He is a strong advocate for the simple yet profound act of TRYING: grandparents going the extra mile in offering forgiveness, compassion, generosity, and humor; in demonstrating fortitude and eschewing all forms of pettiness; and in being open to learning as well as teaching (without preaching). Life is all too short, and we as "the family elders" surely know this better than anybody else in the intergenerational triangle! We can each do our small part to strengthen our families in ways that will be significant and empowering. And in doing so, as older adults, we are sustaining our own physical and mental health and vitality at the same time.

It is difficult—even overwhelming—to try and imagine what our grandchildren's world will look like in the decades to come, with technology and world events developing at such a stunning pace. Jerry demonstrates that time-honored values and cherished family ties need not be lost in the inevitable rush. Instead of resenting change, he gives concrete examples of how technology can create opportunities for simple, consistent connections that strengthen relationships. Grandparents need not settle for being left behind and feeling like we have nothing to offer or that our knowledge, skills, and talents have become irrelevant; we can proactively use technology, for example, to undertake important conversations that will underwrite our legacy. And through his incredibly innovative outline for a "Living Legacy Foundation," Jerry also shows us how to transform our monetary gifts to grandchildren into a learning and bonding experience that is worth its weight in gold.

By ingeniously incorporating dozens of charming and sometimes poignant vignettes contributed by "grandchildren" of all ages, Jerry proves that a caring adult's small gestures, encouraging words, and moral example remain vivid in one's mind for a lifetime. Transmission of family stories helps children blossom into kinder, more embracing adults; this is one of many lessons to be taken from the contributors' uplifting accounts that include grandparents' immigrant struggles, tragedies of history, poverty, and personal trials. Through inspirational stories that are devoid of self-pity and offer only hope, we learn too that individuals are capable of rising out of virtually every sort of disadvantage, to reinvent themselves—and that lives (or families) need not be "ruined" by misfortune. Is there a more valuable lesson for us today?

Brimming with practical wisdom, ageless optimism, and soul-stirring humanity, this uplifting book celebrates the power of grandparenting to transform the lives of individuals and families. The passion, creativity, and candor on its pages will inform and enrich your own grand journey.

I intend to share *The Grandest Love* with my graduate students (in early care and education, mental health, and child welfare) to educate future social-work professionals about the power of honest intergenerational dialogue and discovery, the resilience generated by familial interdependence, and the healing that can come from making family relationships a priority.

I will also read it with my grown children so that together we can create a sacred space to discuss what is truly important to us as a family, to "Teach-and-Learn" with each other, and to become genuinely intentional about the lasting benefits of our family traditions.

There is a saying: "To the world you may be only one person, but to one person you may be the world." There are times in a grandchild's life when we will very likely be their world. Jerry Witkovsky's *The Grandest Love* helps us to be ready for those powerful moments, to embrace them with joy, and to fill all the years in between with meaning, memories, and lessons that endure.

JOAN MALTESE, Ph.D.

*Clinical psychologist **Joan Maltese** is co-founder and executive director of the Child Development Institute in Woodland Hills, California; she has been inspired by young children and the adults who nurture them for over 35 years. She is also on the faculty of California State University at Northridge, where she facilitates the certificate program in Infant/Toddler Family Mental Health.*

INTRODUCTION

THE GRANDEST LOVE:
A LOVE WORTH
"TEACHING-AND-LEARNING" ABOUT

"If a child is to keep alive his inborn sense of wonder, he needs the companionship of at least one adult who can share it, rediscovering with him the joy, excitement and mystery of the world we live in."
—Rachel Carson

"In a brief space the generations of beings are changed, and, like runners, pass on the torches of life."
—Lucretius

Like you, I am a grandparent wildly in love with my grandchildren, who—like yours—are the most amazing, brilliant, attractive, and accomplished grandchildren in all the world.

If you're a grandparent, that sentence undoubtedly makes perfect sense to you. If you're a soon-to-be grandparent, trust me, dear reader, it will make perfect sense to you the moment that cooing bundle is placed in your arms. My late wife, Margaret, and I were blessed to have six of them—three girls and three boys, born between 1983 and 2002.

It didn't surprise me that I became such an ardent grandfather to those enchanting and (let's be honest) sometimes exasperating young people. After all, you're *supposed* to be crazy about your grandchildren. What *did* surprise me was how fascinated I'd become, as a longtime social-work professional, by the unique dynamics of what I've come to call "The Grandest Love" and how deeply convinced I'd become of the grandparent-grandchild relationship's powerful potential to strengthen—even transform—the lives of individuals, families, and communities.

Grandparenting is a sacred trust. In a world characterized by rapid change and shifting social mores, we will remain the grandparents of our children's children, "in sickness and in health, 'til death do us part." That's why I decided to harness sixty-plus years of career expertise, community activism, and parenting, along with three decades of hands-on grandparenting, to write this book.

Grandparents Matter

Thanks to increased longevity, many of us may actually have *40 or more years* to participate in the lives of our grandchildren! And that's not the only good news. Living near each other (or having the means to undertake regular visits) is no longer essential to maintaining close family ties, thanks to burgeoning communications technologies and easy-access social networks that are being embraced by older adults in record numbers. (More on that in chapter 6.)

All this translates into a wealth of opportunities for us to have a profound and enduring impact on our grandchildren's lives. What's more, the benefits of The Grandest Love are a two-way street. Seizing ways to become an actively engaged grandparent helps us maintain vitality and energy, and a powerful sense of purpose and joy, as we age.
(http://ohioline.osu.edu/hygfact/5000/pdf/Benefits_Grandparenting.pdf)

For me, becoming "Grandpa" was the dawn of a new day. Decades ago, during my parenting years, I—like many people— was engaged in demanding work that required long hours away from home and family. As a result, unfortunately, I missed many highlights of my own children's growing-up years. One of the greatest joys of retirement has been the gift of time to participate in my grandchildren's lives—to play board games with them, cheer them on the sports field, teach them how to ride their bikes, pick them up from school, and take them to shows and athletic events. It's been a win-win all around.

Grandchildren Bring Love and Second Chances

I've discovered that The Grandest Love can foster an improved family synergy across the board, enriching my relationship with the *parents* of those amazing grandkids: my daughter, Ellen, and my son, Michael, and their respective spouses. It hasn't always been easy, but we've managed to heal some old wounds and lighten some old baggage. And we are mindful of trying to maintain open, respectful communication and mutual cooperation.

The reality is: when you and your adult offspring are stuck in an unforgiving past, unable to broker a grown-up *détente*, there can be little basking together in the sunshine of the grandchildren. And all three generations, through every season of their lives, will be poorer for it.

The birth of a child heralds a precious time, one that has the power to transform all the adults touched by the experience into more loving people. My hope is that this book will encourage you to be open to such transformations—and even actively try to facilitate them.

Decades of Studying Grandparents

For the last 25 years, The Grandest Love has been the focus of my life and work, researching and lecturing about grandparenting issues, facilitating support groups, and developing community-based programs that allow intergenerational bonds to flourish. Along the way I've listened intently to hundreds of people's stories—grandparents' stories brimming with that special love but often too with a fair amount of conflict and confusion.

Despite the fact that these grandparents were a diverse group, their concerns were startlingly similar, such as the following:

- *"How can I play an active role in nurturing my grandchildren when I've had a less-than-ideal relationship with one—or both—of their parents? How too can we all learn to respect each other's boundaries, across the generations?"*

- *"How do I stay connected to grandchildren who live hundreds of miles away or with ones who live nearby, but whose days are filled with back-to-back activities?"*

- *"With all the stresses and distractions of modern life, and in difficult economic times, how can we as a family unit be truly supportive of each other, enrich each other's lives, and create lasting memories?"*

- *"What is **my** personal legacy to this family? And what can I do to make an impact, to impart something of value, while I'm still around?"*

Sound familiar? These are the challenges and hopes that most of us share.

During my 47 years with a leading Chicago community-center system, I dealt with a number of gut-wrenching family dramas marked by abuse, neglect, or severe dysfunction. Thankfully, the vast majority of us grapple with circumstances that are far less dire. Still, you worry. You want to get this grandparenting thing *right*. And with some thoughtful planning, you almost certainly *will*.

As Stephen R. Covey wrote in his best-selling book, *The 7 Habits of Highly Effective Families*: *"Good families—even great families—are off track 90% of the time! The key is that they have a sense of destination. They know what the 'track' looks like. And they keep coming back to it time and time again."*

A "Family Vision" of the Grandest Love

No family, even the most caring, the most privileged, is immune from being thrown off their track. There are any number of reasons: divorce, money problems, health crises, geographic distance, religious/political differences, child-rearing issues (especially in regard to youngsters who take scary detours on the road to adulthood), and more. In the final chapter (chapter 10) of *The Grandest Love*, I list some useful resources for families dealing with difficult situations. In the nine preceding chapters, I focus primarily on **ways that we grandparents can take the lead in building a solid foundation of love, trust, and communication across the generations.** That's what sustains everyone when the tough stuff, inevitably, comes their way, and it makes the good times all the more sweet.

How do we become that strong, connected, on-track family? Even when everyone has the best of intentions, there are so often old hurts and unproductive behaviors that stand in the way.

In chapter 2, I'll provide simple tools to help you develop a **Family Vision Statement** rooted in your shared values, interests, and goals. Investing some time in a vision statement and in the short, engaging **"Journaling Expeditions"** that follow each chapter can help you to lead *your* family in embracing the positive and discarding the negative.

Through my own family's Vision Statement, we discovered our common ground: **a family culture centered on "Teaching-and-Learning."**

That's when a family undertakes a conscious effort to routinely share key interests, core beliefs, and favorite activities with one another as a way of building respect for each individual, bringing the generations closer, and broadening each other's worldview.

What's So Great about Teaching and Learning?

A Teaching-and-Learning paradigm can offer a way out for families trapped in a maze of unfulfilling interactions.

In its unhappiest manifestations, it's an all-too-familiar intergenerational triangle, a rigid hierarchy in which Grandma and Grandpa are viewed as being critical and controlling, and unduly focused on the "respect" they feel is due them. Their adult children still carry the burden of resentments from their own childhoods, which only compound the stresses of making a living in a weak economy and raising young families in a complex, rapidly changing world. And *their* children, as they're growing up, reveal little of their inner lives to the people who love them the most—because they assume that their ideas and experiences will be dismissed by judgmental adults whose beliefs are antiquated anyway.

In many of our families, of course, daily living isn't quite *so* fraught; but we know, deep down, things aren't what they could be or what we once hoped they'd be. Sometimes there doesn't seem to be much to talk about, regardless of how often or how rarely we actually see each other or sit down together. Quiet resentments, disappointments, and misunderstandings persist, because nobody feels comfortable to speak honestly, from the heart, without fear of censure. As the family elders, we may look back on our efforts to foster the proverbial "roots and wings" and ask ourselves, *could this family's roots be deeper? Could our wings be stronger?*

Gratifyingly, people in Teaching-and-Learning families have, for the most part, unusually fluid roles within the family structure. Each individual, regardless of age or "resume," is empowered by the knowledge that he or she has **something of value to contribute to the collective** and something to take from it too. Closed-minded thinking and dated stereotypes, hurtful labels and old bitterness, can give way to knowing, enjoying, and admiring each other for who you are today and for who you are striving to become. Everyone, the youngest to the oldest, feels heard. This doesn't mean that everyone always agrees. But most of the time, in families, when disagreements mushroom into serious conflicts, it's because one party or another—or both—did not feel *heard*.

Teaching-and-Learning has proven to be so positive for my family, and for others who have undertaken it, that I'm highlighting it as an overarching concept built into every single chapter. **A Teaching-and-Learning model can actually jumpstart all the processes in this book, invigorating not only your family relationships but also virtually every aspect of your life.** And I'm talking about truly life-changing processes (which we'll examine more fully, going forward), like learning how to create a healthy balance between independence and interdependence, defuse anger, build trust and achieve forgiveness.

Youth Gets a Voice, Elders Retain Theirs

It takes some time and effort for Teaching-and-Learning to become ingrained in a family culture. The benefits, however, become apparent very quickly, as a trifecta of steadily mounting respect:

- *Grandparents* are able to impart wisdom without lording over the rest of the family; they show themselves to be flexible thinkers who are open to new ideas.

- *Adult children* feel empowered and aren't as liable to regress to knee-jerk defensiveness toward their parents or to become overly authoritarian with their children.

- *Youngsters* who are made to feel that their voices matter are less likely to tune out the voices of others. They develop pride and confidence in their own ideas and accomplishments, and aren't so quick to view their elders as prehistoric purveyors of obsolete notions.

And those disagreements? They just aren't automatically as aggressively *personal*. Typically, teaching-and-learning families will debate vigorously about *ideas*. **And when nobody's on the attack, nobody's on the defensive.**

There's nothing like being an avid "learner" about your grandchildren's world. New ideas are energizing, revitalizing; they are as essential to keeping the aging brain sharp and elastic as exercise is to the aging body.

Of course, we also play an essential role as teachers. In previous eras, this was a given; grandparents were regarded—not to mention revered and obeyed—as the all-knowing chieftains of the family. Well, we've come a long way from "Father (or Grandfather) Knows Best"; and in a great many ways, that's for the best. But sometimes it feels like the pendulum has swung too sharply in the opposite direction, in a culture that seems to value youthful appearance, achievement and ideas above all others. As high-tech entrepreneur Bryan Goldberg admitted not long ago, in a blog post for the Silicon Valley-based website PandoDaily: **"We live twice as long as we used to, but we are ten times quicker to write people off as irrelevant or too old to ever achieve anything great."**
(http://pandodaily.com/2013/01/18/a-world-safe-for-39-year-olds/)

By sharing our experiences—and making new ones—with our grandchildren, we teach them to value every era of life. Our lives and relationships, individually and collectively, are the fabric of the world they've inherited. They can learn a great deal from our successes and no less from our failures. And think of all the stories that we accumulate over a lifetime! If you're anything like me, you've got a whole arsenal of them—some hilarious, some bittersweet, and most of them, in one way or another, highly instructive.

In a storytelling class I recently took, the professor shared this quote: "When an elderly person dies, a library burns to the ground." As grandparents, our goal should be that not a single volume should remain unread on those shelves. This is the family lore our grandchildren will take with them into the future.

An Innovative Approach to a "Living Legacy"

As it happens, *I'm* the "relic" who conceived of what my family considers one of the most exciting shared activities we've ever undertaken: the Witkovsky Living Legacy Foundation.

In a nutshell: like many of you, I was eager to help underwrite some of my grandkids' dream projects, educational pursuits, and travels. Plus, I wanted to be around to see their ventures bear fruit. In chapter 8, I'll tell you how it's been working for us, and I'll also provide you with **a step-by-step plan on how to create a Living Legacy Foundation for *your* family**, tailored to your own means and goals. It's an original concept I'm thrilled to share.

The Value of Trying

Is it "work" to sustain The Grandest Love? Sometimes (as with most things worth having) it is. A few of the activities in this book, frankly, may strike you or some of your family members as outside your comfort zones, abilities, or interests. And that's fine; I'm a teacher, not a preacher. Based on my experiences as a clinician, however, I'd like to propose one single word: **TRY.** Try something a little different, do *just a little more*. The reality is, no matter how diligently we work on our relationships, none of them come with guarantees; ultimately, there may be only modest ripples of change within your family. What I *can* promise unequivocally **is that the very act of *trying* to be a more conscious, involved, Teaching-and-Learning grandparent will enhance your well-being and quell a good deal of whatever loneliness you may experience.**

And let's not forget about having FUN. In chapter 7, you'll see how memorable experiences don't necessarily require lots of money, and that wonderful relationships aren't necessarily the product of lots of togetherness. Sometimes the smallest loving gesture, the right words at the right time, can endure for a lifetime.

Presenting: "The Grandchildren Speak"

Don't just take only my word for it; this book is peppered with quotations from well-known voices, both ancient and modern, upholding the importance of grandparents. And I'm gratified to call your attention to a section of each chapter, called "The Grandchildren Speak," and to introduce you to 49 individuals, representing a diversity of ages and backgrounds, who submitted stirring personal stories about a grandparent's impact on their lives.

A number of the contributors are professional (or aspiring) writers; many are not. Some of their reflections are charming, some are immensely uplifting, and a few are cautionary and sad. Interestingly, among our respondents, a disproportionate number were grandchildren of Holocaust survivors. Their deeply poignant reflections illustrate that even families marked by epic trauma and loss have the capacity to regenerate and become wellsprings for inspiration and positive living.

I hope that this chorus of voices, together with my own, will send forth the message that The Grandest Love really matters, and that a grandparent's light—whether it shines only briefly or for many years—can illuminate a family's path for generations to come.

THE GRANDCHILDREN SPEAK

A LIFE OF INSATIABLE CURIOSITY

Jayendra Bhatt was a rickety old man at first glance. He would careen down our suburban sidewalk using his cane as if it were a comedic prop to make us grandchildren laugh. But "Dada" wasn't rickety, neither in body nor in spirit. In his native India, he had been a scholar, a philosopher, a teacher—and a boxer. And although he appeared delicate in his old age, he still had the muscles to prove it.

Educated by the British in his native India, Dada would still ask us to "make haste" when he wanted us to hurry and "take heed" when he wanted us to listen, even after twenty years of living with us in California. He always had a book in hand, and every birthday card came with a classic novel, biography, book of poetry, or textbook. He had read and loved them all. He had flipped through his books to give me my name, choosing a Sanskrit word, *Foram,* meaning "fragrance"—a name as unique as me being the first girl to be born in eight generations of his family. Even in his last moments, before dying of a heart attack in bed, he took his final breaths with a paperback resting on his chest.

After his passing, reading his books—pulled off shelves and out of nightstands and from under beds—became a way for our family to remember him. For me, it became a way to honor him, to inherit his restless pursuit of understanding life through literature. Today, I fill my walls with books—his and mine—and remember.

While his hours, days, and years were filled by his insatiable curiosity, Dada believed that true happiness ultimately came only from simplicity, from peace within the heart after realizing the world around us. Indeed, every day he would ask me, "Are you happy?" I would respond, "Yeah, Dada, I'm happy." Then he would smile and say, "Good, that's all."

FORAM BHATT (24)
Canoga Park, California

PANCAKES

My grandmother made me pancakes whenever I visited her. Without fail, I would arrive to the smell of hot butter and the sight of a yellow

Bisquick box on the kitchen counter. Even if I wasn't hungry, she would sit me down for a heaping plate. Every time.

"Mimi" knew what I didn't: that I desperately needed something dependable in my life. I was seven, and my parents' divorce had shaken my family and left them both helpless. I believe I could have been driven into terrible habits or a hopeless future. But she gave me the semblance of a strong foundation, even if I saw her no more than once a month.

Those pancakes became something to look forward to, a glint of hope in a wider story of despair. Mimi and her pancakes provided me with the stability I needed, something warm and nourishing in days that felt dark and cold.

JESSE J. RABBITS (22)
Harrisburg, Pennsylvania

A GRANDFATHER'S GREETING

Everyone who knew Eddie could recognize him when he answered the phone:

"YYELLO!"

That jovial, bellowing greeting typified Eddie and his outlook. With that single, common word, his enthusiasm and zeal would zap across the country into the receiver, wherever I was. All at once, it said: "Tell me what's new. Tell me what you think. I can't wait to hear."

It was his optimism and excitement, his confidence and his constancy condensed into one word, and it was the first word I always heard him say.

SANDERS WITKOW (28)
Westport, Connecticut

THE MANTLE OF STORYTELLING

Zeyde was always a storyteller. Throughout my childhood, stories trickled out of him and sometimes out of his children in unpredictable times and places. Stories of the frigid Christmas in Auschwitz, when he siphoned piles of apple and potato peels from the kitchen of a Nazi officers' feast to the barracks of his starving friends. Stories of New

Year's Eve, 1946, when Zeyde danced with a beautiful woman at a party in a Displaced Persons camp—the same woman he had spotted on a soup line, immediately after the camps were liberated, only now a tall, red-headed officer was wooing her. Zeyde bought the officer round after round of drinks, until he was sure this woman would stay in his arms forever.

Zeyde and Bubbie held fast to each other for the next fifty years; when she battled ovarian cancer, he taught himself to cook like a professional chef, and fed her tenderly until the end.

Zeyde made me a storyteller too. I wrote about him in my college essay, and he is the wise, tenacious grandfather who always finds his way into my fiction. I shared his tales before a group of fifty teenagers in the barracks of Auschwitz-Birkenau, 65 years after he'd slept there. I told them how he smiled like a constellation of faraway stars as he described the faces of prisoners who watched him, that Christmas night, wheel in that wheelbarrow, remove a tarp, then some tools, and then a mini-Everest of apple and potato peels.

Now, at 92, Zeyde seldom speaks of the past, but speaks of the future. Every time I come home from college, we sit together in his living room in the Bronx, and he quizzes me about employment and marriage. In his arsenal of conversation topics, talk of history has been neutered: *Jacob, did you know that Russia has twelve time zones? How about that Germany produces five of the world's top ten cars?* And he still has dreams. At the ripe young age of 90, he asked my dad and me to accompany him on an epic riverboating journey down the Mississippi to the Gulf of Mexico.

There will be no riverboat; almost all family gatherings now take place on sea of curly orange carpeting that covers his living room, because leaving home can be disorienting for him. But the man still has pleasures. Recently, over a game of five-card stud, he beckoned me to the bottles of Courvoisier he secretes in a cabinet near the front door. *"You want something real nice to drink, Jacob? It goes down . . ."* and he held the air with his hand and pursed his lips to indicate an immaculate smoothness.

"What are you talking about in there, Mr. Kaufman?" his aide, Jill, called coyly from the other room. He gave me another one of those smiles that could illuminate the world, as he raised his teacup with an *"ahhhh."* If my parents hadn't summoned me to leave just then, I'm pretty sure that Zeyde would have offered his usual toast (*"I'm gonna tell you, everyone shall be healthy, we will be here, next year, together . . . L'Chaim!"*), and the two of us would have gotten good and drunk together. But I told him to save the bottles for our time on the riverboat.

In the car, my dad asked what had prompted Zeyde to dip into the Courvoisier and to reveal his stash to me. I didn't have an answer. "The whole thing was pretty spontaneous," I shrugged. My mother said: "Maybe he was remembering some night of drunken revelry and poker in the bungalow colony we stayed at when I was a kid." Or maybe he was remembering the night of the dance, when he captured his dream girl. As if the man needs a reason to celebrate.

Each time I retell his stories, every time his words spill from my lips, they play out slightly differently: some details are lost, a few are embellished, and some are just wrong. In part, I'm pained by this, but I'll bet Zeyde never told the exact same story twice either. I think that's just how people keep stories alive.

JACOB KOSE (23)
New York, New York

Journaling Expedition:

Introduction

1. **Is there an anecdote you recall that encapsulates your own grandparent's legacy?**

_____
_____
_____
_____
_____

2. **What lesson(s) did you take from this story when you first heard (or experienced) it? And today, in hindsight, do you see it differently? If so, how?**

_____
_____
_____
_____

_____

_____

_____

_____

_____

_____

_____

_____

3. Is there a story from your own life that you think might encapsulate a portion of your own legacy or "message" to your grandchildren?

_____

_____

_____

_____

_____

_____

_____

_____

_____

_____

CHAPTER I

MY STORY: AN ONGOING JOURNEY TOWARD GRAND CONNECTION

---

*"Perfect love sometimes does not come until
the first grandchild."*

—Welsh Proverb

*"Just look at my face. It's an extraordinary experience. All
of my friends who are grandparents have been saying, just
wait, a bit cynically, but it's just extraordinary. You feel like
a child again yourself. Just walking on air."*

—Blythe Danner

I experienced that feeling of "walking on air," the one I call
The Grandest Love, the moment I laid eyes on each of my
grandchildren, starting with Jessica, born in 1983. Given my
many years in the social-work field, I had long been cognizant
of the important role that grandparents and extended families
play in a child's life and development. So you might assume
that my determination to be the very best grandfather I could be
would have kicked in immediately.

But that's not quite how it happened.

Like many of you today, I was very busy. My grandparenting years started when I was still in the prime of my career; even once I had retired, I was still quite active—and remain so—as a consultant and a community volunteer. Then there was a matter of distance. My son, Michael, and his family live in Madison, Wisconsin, a three-hour drive from my home in Chicago. Ellen, my daughter, started out raising her family in a neighboring Chicago suburb; she, her husband, and their two daughters relocated to Los Angeles in 2001.

And there was another kind of distance too. Oh, we all got along quite well when we got together several times a year, but—like in many families—along with a lot of obvious love and affection, there were areas of wariness and contention that probably had been smoldering quietly since Michael and Ellen were teenagers.

Until Margaret, my wife, became ill with cancer, she was a tirelessly creative and fun grandmother, always ready to pull out her craft materials or to play a spirited game of Scrabble. I wasn't a much different grandfather, I suppose, than I was a father, which meant I was very caring and, did I mention, very busy?

Many people have candidly and courageously shared their personal stories in this book. This chapter will start with my own.

A Crisis Hits Home

It's been a grandparenting journey of more than three decades, but I'll begin in 1992, on the beautiful fall day when Margaret and I learned that our grandson Benny, just two years old, had suddenly taken ill and needed to be hospitalized. We immediately jumped into our car and drove to Madison to see how we could support our son's young family.

During those difficult days and nights in the pediatric ICU, I had the feeling that the four of us—Margaret and I, and Benny's frightened parents—were suspended together in another dimension. Stripped of our daily preoccupations and petty disagreements, we were remarkably in sync, bound by a common purpose. We needed to operate together as an effective team to do everything we could for Benny and his big brother, eight-year-old Ethan.

I have to say that we were quite the team. By truly listening to each other, focusing on our joint mission, and working to our individual strengths, we mapped out a workable plan: who picks up Ethan at school, who stays with Benny, who gets the groceries, who fields the nonstop phone calls, and so on. Without fear, embarrassment, or recrimination, we were able to be honest with each other too about who might need a break and who might need a hug, who yearned for an encouraging word, and who wanted to be left alone.

Throughout Benny's illness and subsequent recuperation, as the circumstances changed, so did our plan.

After the ordeal had passed, I was indescribably relieved that Benny was doing so well and proud of how each of us had managed to step up to the plate. Yet one thing nagged at me. I wondered: *Why does it always take events like this one to make people genuinely attuned to each other's needs? Why should it take near-tragedy to remind us how much we rely on and value each other?* Of course, these are the questions that most of us ask ourselves at critical life junctures. All too often, however, after that crisis passes, so does our resolve.

And sure enough, as Benny, blessedly, returned to full health, our busy family returned to business as usual.

Each Family: A Little Civilization

As the years flew by, and we hurtled into a new millennium, the grandchildren grew, and more of them were born, and we only got busier. Oh, life was good—but still, it sometimes felt like one big pressure cooker. The trauma of 9/11 and escalating global terrorism. The war in Iraq. Alarming manifestations of climate change and economic instability. Revelations of corruption in our most trusted institutions—financial, governmental, religious, scientific. Technological advances that, while exciting, seemed to be evolving too fast for us to grasp them! One couldn't help but think of the classic line from "Casablanca": that the problems of a few little people "don't amount to a *hill of beans* in this crazy world."

Yet this was the crazy world in which my grandkids were coming of age, the world they would someday inherit. Their parents—my dear children—were doing the very best they could, but I could tell it was often a struggle. I wanted to help, but I knew that there were boundaries that needed to be respected; I just wasn't certain where they were.

Someone once wrote that each family is like a little civilization. A unique, fragile little civilization that must be strong if it is to withstand the disruptions that continually imperil its existence.

I knew I couldn't change the world, which seemed to be spinning faster and faster. But maybe I could take a shot at changing *our little corner of it*, making it warmer, kinder, more fulfilling.

The question was how? It would take a couple of more years before I seized upon the answer.

A (Quiet) Wake-Up Call

This time, the impetus was nowhere near as dramatic as Benny's illness. I was visiting Ellen and her family; and I volunteered to pick up her younger daughter, Kathryn (who we mostly call "Katie"), then 13, at the end of her school day.

"So how was school?" I asked her, by rote.

This time, Katie refused to give me a rote answer. She deposited her backpack on the ground and resolutely folded her arms. "Grandpa," she said sharply, "I'm *more* than just a student, you know!"

Of *course*, I knew! But did I, really?

I knew that Katie's world went beyond the academic subjects scribbled on her binder covers, beyond the soccer games I'd inquire about diligently. She had a rich, deepening life of the mind, full of dreams and convictions, doubts and fears; and now she was inviting me in to share it through a small window *that might soon close*. Standard queries, preachy advice, the check in the mail for birthdays and holidays — these weren't the tickets for admission to Katie's world, or to any other youngster's world, for that matter. I knew I couldn't kid myself any longer. Despite my loving intentions, I had to admit to myself that I was not the grandfather I'd hoped to be.

And I had so much more to offer! Throughout my career, I was privileged to have mentored generations of young people, from my early years as a camp director, though the decades during which I supervised hundreds of young clinicians and group-workers throughout the greater Chicago area. I knew I had made a real difference in their lives because so many of them have, gratifyingly, stayed in touch and told me so. And mentoring was by no means a one-way street. I have learned a great deal from the legions of fine young folks who have passed through my life!

I had a reputation as a leader who knew how to empower others to reach their potential. So why wasn't I *consciously* leading and empowering my *own* family the same way? And why wasn't I embracing all that my own children and grandchildren could offer me to enlarge my world-view?

"I'm more than just a student, Grandpa!" It was, on the face of it, an innocuous little jibe, the words of a young teen who was grumpy after a tiring day.

But it hit its mark like a laser.

A Look in the Mirror

In the days that followed Katie's outburst, I thought back to the exceptional synergy that had reigned during Benny's illness.

Obviously, most of life doesn't have the drama or clarity of purpose of an ICU. When it comes to the enormously complex dance of human relations, how can we possibly know what's in another person's heart? What is their true hierarchy of goals? What are their struggles, their convictions, their deepest yearnings? We can't know, unless we actively seek to find out. And wasn't that process of "finding out" a basic tenet of my own profession?

It dawned on me that this seasoned social worker needed to look deep into the soul of his *own* family unit, and begin applying what he knew to be effective models to foster genuine communication, connection, and growth.

As a supervisor, I had always emphasized the importance of developing a customized plan of action. Call it "Social Work 101": first, identify a group's needs and objectives by asking the right questions of all of its members and really listening to their individual answers. Ensure that every individual's unique strengths and weaknesses are taken into account. Codify the issues at hand—i.e., *write things down*—so they're not left to memory or to chance; and so that, one day, the parties are able to look back at what was written and get a true picture of how far they've come. And take immense care that all interactions are rooted in courtesy, compassion, and respect.

Time and again, I had witnessed how these "best practices" had been life preservers that helped drowning families, despite major obstacles, to *survive.*

Applying them, in some fashion, to reasonably happy families—families like my own—could be the key to making them *thrive.*

All along, I had been grandparenting solely *by instinct and habit* when what I *really* needed to do was to grandparent *consciously, deliberately, and by design.*

Family Meetings Change the Paradigm

I realized that the first thing I needed to do was to examine my interactions with my adult children. This was no small hurdle. There was an abundance of love between us, but there were unresolved issues too. When we disagreed on something or simply felt tired and short-tempered, our default mode was a hopelessly outdated one, harkening back to the days when they were the combative kids and I was their authoritarian dad. This was baggage we needed to shed if we were to effectively nurture and guide the *next* generation, and to serve as worthy examples for them!

I was convinced that we, as a family, had what it took to safeguard our "little civilization" from life's inevitable storms. But a strong home requires a strong foundation. And like any architects, we needed to begin with a blueprint.

I proposed that the next time we all gathered for a holiday celebration, we set aside some time for a formalized Family Meeting, a couple of hours with a planned agenda that would include guided discussion and writing. The two holidays we traditionally spent together—one religious, one secular—were both, in fact, rife for the deeper interactions and "relationship building" I envisioned. Thanksgiving is a natural juncture for all Americans, youngest to oldest, to reflect on what we are thankful for and on what we might wish for ourselves and for each other in the coming season. And on Passover, the centerpiece of the Seder dinner is the recitation of the Haggadah, the annual retelling "from generation to generation" of the ancient Hebrews' exodus from Egypt. Its epic themes of freedom, redemption, and renewal are a springboard for fascinating values discussions, both personal and political.

Did we engage in these kinds of discussions *before* undertaking Family Meetings? Sure we did. But coming up with carefully considered topics and writing prompts helped us to focus and enrich our (all-too-rare) time together, much like a diligent teacher's lesson plan will enhance a class's learning experience.

The Agenda: Our Values, Our Vision

As one might expect, there was plenty of eye-rolling when I announced, that first Thanksgiving weekend, that it was time to turn off the TV and take a break from the leftovers and chit-chat, to convene in the living room. When I actually started distributing paper and pencils so everyone could fill out a Family Vision Quiz, there were audible groans! Most of them went along with it, I've no doubt, solely to indulge good ol' Dad, a.k.a. Grandpa. This didn't exactly thrill me, but I barreled ahead anyway! What kind of an example would I be if I didn't persevere when something really mattered to me?

I knew I couldn't live with myself if I didn't demonstrate the value of TRYING, something I'd espoused to my family and to my staff at work, all my life.

The youngest ones ran off to play, at first. But I noticed that they eventually came back into the room to burrow into their parents' or cousins' laps and seemed to be listening attentively. Pretty soon they began piping up during our free-flowing conversation.

The results of our Family Values Quiz highlighted some things I had already felt about how we interacted at our best. Discussing important topics like social justice, education, and religion was clearly a natural platform for our family, even its junior members. The quiz drove home that all of us appeared to relish both **teaching and learning** according to our individual abilities, knowledge, and interests. We didn't need to share the same passions or beliefs to be brought closer by them. We could grow, individually and as a unit, by "showing and telling" what it was we loved, by listening, by asking questions, and (where needed) by showing support.

As an outgrowth of the values quiz, at our next Family Meeting, we decided to develop a statement of the family life we aspired to and called it "Our Family Vision." In the next chapter, I'll give you some pointers on how to do all this for your own family, to whatever extent and in whatever fashion works for you.

Our Family Vision (Witkovsky Edition)

This family can be:

- *Our launch pad* . . . where we soar from in exploration; where we return, again and again, to share treasures amassed through growth and risk taking; where we go forth to better our own lives and the lives of others.

- *Our safe haven* . . . where we can share our hopes and dreams, and trust that they will never be minimized or belittled; where we can fail, but are never made to feel like failures.

- *Our wellspring* . . . where love is nurtured and nurtures in return; our sustenance in times of both joy and sorrow, its capacity continually replenished—even enlarged—by healthy conflict and vigorous debate.

- *Our spiritual refuge* . . . where we can retreat to sort out confusion, and heal from pain, in an atmosphere of tenderness and understanding.

- *Our support system* . . . where we are comfortable asking for and receiving help; where we mobilize our collective assets (knowledge and insights, talents and love) to steadfastly aid each other in meeting life's challenges.

- *Our anchor* . . . where a profound sense of belonging becomes the strong and steady center of our being.

- *Our roots and wings* . . . where communal responsibility is cherished and individual freedom is celebrated.

Over the course of the next few years, the Family Meeting became woven into the fabric of our holiday gatherings. There were still groans from certain quarters when the paper and pencils came out. And rest assured, folks, at this stage of the game, I often shove them back into the drawer.

But I think we all felt that the planned-for meetings helped us turn a corner. We became practiced and more comfortable at the *intentional* act of airing the issues that mattered to us. Our conversations became deeper, more engaging, and more revealing, whether debating weighty philosophical concepts, or discussing our shared enthusiasm for camping, travel, and football. (Naturally, things still get heated from time to time, especially between the Green Bay Packers diehards and the Chicago Bears contingent.)

Connections Deepen

The improved synergy spills over to our interactions all year long. At birthday celebrations, along with having the usual candles and cake, the celebrant shares thoughts about the highlights of his or her year (or decade). We started sending group emails highlighting articles or books we're reading, and sharing our reactions with each other. Several years back, after I came across a Holocaust memoir I found extremely affecting, I bought a copy for every grandchild and had it signed and personalized by the author. I believed they too would be moved by it, and this opened the door for discussion of the book and the important topic.

And there have been wonderful shared vacations too—like South Carolina and Georgia, to relax on the beach—because those are the activities that all of us enjoy.

That said, our family, like most, hasn't been immune from financial fluctuations and periods of unemployment. We take care to plan outings that don't put undue strain on anybody's budget—and our circumstances are sometimes quite disparate. Some of our very best times have been barbeques in the backyard on summer evenings, and afternoons together in front of the TV, watching a big game.

I confess, though, that there have been times when I was guided more by The Grandest Love than by my accountant's advice. I'm not a man of significant wealth, but I worked hard and saved carefully. Helping to underwrite **shared experiences that create lifelong memories** for my children and their children is just about the best investment and the most meaningful gift I can imagine. I do not advocate grandparents going beyond their means to heap largesse upon their families, even when "the other grandparents" are able to do so (a not-uncommon scenario). I do, however, heartily recommend that grandparents who are wondering what to buy kids and grandkids for birthdays or holidays, consider providing experiences, which are "forever," instead of piling on "things" that all too quickly become obsolete.

Giving Back

My family members and I are very conscious that we are privileged to be able to share the things we do. This awareness is part of our shared Family Vision that values "bettering the lives of others." Each of us prioritizes volunteerism in our various communities, and this has emerged as a powerful topic of Teaching-and-Learning whenever we get together. Ellen, my daughter, currently serves as president of her synagogue, an activity to which she devotes a great deal of time, effort, and textual study. We have all benefited from her teaching us about this major undertaking; she benefits from our questions and insights.

Even the younger grandkids understand that giving back is a central component of how we see our family. From a very early age, they participated with their parents in community cleanups and the like and (as discussed in chapter 8) have learned to set aside a portion of their money for charity.

Meetings in Good Times and Bad

When life gets tough, having a strongly connected family unit becomes a gift beyond measure. Never was this more apparent than in the years during and after Margaret's final illness. (She died in August of 2003.) Family Meetings provided a forum for us to share painful thoughts and emotions that may have been too difficult to air had we not gotten some "practice" at being open and vulnerable around each other.

Our enhanced communication wasn't only a balm, emotionally; it was a godsend, operationally. As a caregiver, I don't know what I would have done without my children's strong support, practical advice, and words of love from near and far. Our granddaughter Jessica moved from California for an entire summer, before returning to college, to live with us and help us. I will never forget her compassion.

I'm convinced that the loyalty and sensitivity everyone displayed during those grief-laden times were cultivated by the important discussions we'd launched in "normal" times. And thus it continues. Working toward mutual respect and understanding, and trust and forgiveness, is an ongoing process. Sometimes it's a joy and at other times a struggle.

Family Meetings provide a forum for those important discussions. Two years after Margaret's death, I began dating a wonderful woman who has been my companion ever since. We met in a support group for bereaved spouses. I knew it might be strange for the rest of the family to think about me having a lady-friend, and that they might have some mixed feelings about it because of Margaret. My blossoming relationship became our meeting's agenda; we shared a heart-to-heart talk, a few laughs, and a few tears.

Probably the most powerful agenda of any Family Meeting we've ever had also took place a couple of years after Margaret's death. We resolved to do everything in our power to ensure that no member of our family, regardless of financial resources, would ever lack for needed medical care or psychological support, that no young person would be prevented from attending college or trade school, and that no elderly person would be forced to live out his or her days in poverty.

I realize that these are awfully broad statements, given the immense complexity of such situations. But identifying and affirming our shared values and convictions is an essential starting point. Now it is our task to lay foundations under them.

Welcoming Differing Points of View

Striving to become more connected as a family doesn't mean that everyone is obliged to see things the same way. For example, not all of my family members see a *deliberate* commitment to Teaching-and-Learning as being central to our family's synergy. Says my daughter, Ellen, herself a social worker, and the vice president of a large nonprofit organization:

> *I'm not so conscious of an intentional Teaching-And-Learning model to our interactions the way my dad is, frankly. As a parent and an aunt, a daughter, a wife and a sister, I try to be present in the lives of my loved ones — to show interest in what they are passionate about, and to share with them what I'm passionate about.*

> *I think about my talent for quilting, for example, and about the gifts I've made for each of them — but I don't think of that as an act of teaching, really. There's nothing intentional other then showing love through my creativity.*

> *I have learned to watch the human beings I care about discover themselves and grow, without trying to impose my own dreams or values on them. I think they are all very cool people with a lot to offer, and I enjoy being around them!*

And what about my personal prescription of plenty of talk and togetherness as being key to a healthy extended family? My son, Michael, who is a psychiatrist, sometimes needs to remind me that it is also important to value and respect each individual's desire for periods of silence, solitude, and separateness. Trees do not grow if they stand too close and are constantly in each other's shadow. Neither do people or families.

As a big fan of frequent, ongoing communication, I can't say that an appreciation for silence is tops on my list! But learning from my family *is*. Fashioning a Teaching-and-Learning family dynamic means being open to viewpoints that may not come naturally. I am grateful for this paradigm because it helps me to not feel insulted or defensive when my ideas or behaviors are challenged.

Grandchildren as Valued Partners in Teaching-and-Learning

As the years have passed, and the grandchildren are branching out, I see Teaching-and-Learning as supplanting, in the best possible way, the judgmentalism to which many families (ours included) easily fall prey. When global politics become a topic of discussion at Witkovsky gatherings, or the theme of one of our group email threads, our teacher is often Benny, who has been interning at a leading Washington, D.C., social-action organization. We aren't required to share Benny's political convictions to be fascinated by his highly sophisticated, insider's point of view. On matters of theology, we alternately defer to and debate with his brother, Ethan, a third-year rabbinical student. Our business guru is Kathryn, who works in the marketing department of a major, Las Vegas-based resort. Jessica is an animal wrangler in Hollywood, recently returned from an African safari. We're all agog over the wildlife photos she posts on Facebook!

Even the youngest children can proudly teach and learn, if given the opportunity. Merete shared with us the step-by-step process of learning to read from a Torah scroll for her Bat Mitzvah last fall. And Aidan presented me with his fourth-grade reading list so I can read some of the books too. Not only will I have the enjoyment of revisiting some classics of my own youth, but I'll discover some *new* classics as well. And Aidan and I can have stimulating conversations that go beyond that listless one that jolted me out of complacency a decade ago:

"So how's school going?"

"Fine, Grandpa."

That's right: I know that Aidan is "more than just a student." We all do.

Not long ago, a new voice was added to our chorus. On March 18, 2012, I had the pleasure and privilege of watching Ethan joined in marriage to his radiant bride, Erin Beser, an educator. I knew I was witnessing more than the union of two beautiful young souls; I was watching the circle of life, within our family, begin a momentous new turn for each of us.

Reaping the Rewards

In late 2009, I asked my four older grandchildren to write a letter about what they believed they had learned from Margaret and me through the years. (The letters appear in chapter 9.) I was touched by their thoughtful responses, but one of them didn't start out very promisingly. It was from Benny, then 17, who (with his short-lived medical crisis long behind him) had grown into a very healthy, very independent-minded young man.

"Dear Grandpa," he began . . . and it seemed to go downhill from there.

Benny went on to declare that he wasn't terribly impressed with our Family Meetings, with the books I'd given him, or my efforts to teach him how to ride a bike, among other things.

I wasn't sure whether to feel hurt or angry, and I began to ponder where I'd gone wrong! But then I read his closing paragraph:

"It is the commitment to an idea that I have learned from you. I have watched you redefine your quest, as you have been turned down, encouraged and questioned. I have seen you take some criticisms and reject others. And I have learned how to explore an idea that you know has some inherent truth but that you are ceaselessly morphing for the

best way to define, understand and present. I don't know what my idea will be yet, but I hope I own it with the same conviction."

How did this make me feel?

I'll tell you: ABSOLUTELY GRAND.

THE GRANDCHILDREN SPEAK

TELL IT LIKE IT IS

My grandmother, Marilyn Tanzer, was a knockout.

"I used to be a very pretty girl, you know," she would regularly announce to her four grandchildren. Grandma was voted "Prettiest Face" back in high school and had pictures to prove it. But nobody needed proof.

Legend had it that the first time she trained her long-lashed eyes on her future husband, Sidney, she ran straight into a closet and refused to come out. She was aghast at the thought of going out in public with him. Sidney was decked out in waist-high, bright yellow rain boots, and that was just not acceptable for the glamorous Marilyn. But they were married for over fifty years, until her death in 2011, so I guess they worked things out.

Her beauty was outshone only by her spunk. She often recounted how she decided to get working papers at age fourteen, falsifying her age so she could earn money of her own—which she spent mostly on riding Coney Island's famed roller coaster, the Thunderbolt, as often as she pleased. So I like to think that my own crazy New York City misadventures—armed (until last year) with my very own fake ID—were inspired by Grandma.

She taught me that you don't have to take it when you think someone is treating you shabbily and that there's no substitute for "telling it like it is." She did just that all her life, combining scathing honesty with blistering wit. Even just before she died, she told a nurse she was unhappy with, "I'm gonna beat you up on Avenue U!"

I'd like to think that Grandma's wit, her edge, her fierce commitment to honesty even in the most uncomfortable of situations, have all rubbed off on me. As an aspiring journalist, I'm convinced that having such a tough cookie as a role model will serve me very well.

MYLES TANZER (22)
Staten Island, New York

STAYING CONNECTED—THANKS TO SELMA

Six-and-a-half days a week, Grandma Selma toiled alongside Grandpa Fred, running a New Jersey boarding house. Sunday afternoons, however, were sacred. That's when she and Grandpa visited their only child and his family—my dad, mom, two brothers and me. She'd come bearing a large roasting pan filled with savory beef or chicken, and reveled in watching us enjoy her cooking.

Grandma treasured the extended family, too, and made sure that birthdays and holidays were always spent in the company of nephews and cousins. These ties were kept strong even after my family moved to California in 1973, with Grandma and Grandpa joining us six months later.

Truthfully, I'd need a diagram to figure out how I'm related to some of these cousins, yet they are among the people I cherish most. We do our best to stay in touch—Facebook has really helped with that. Even when time and money have been scarce, we've prioritized sharing each other's happy occasions like weddings and Bar/Bat Mitzvahs. Because of this, my own child, age 13, is now forging relationships with the children of my cousins, despite, in some cases, living at opposite ends of the country.

Grandma Selma has been gone for close to fifteen years, but I know she'd be delighted that the bonds she worked so hard to foster have not only endured—they have flourished.

NANCY SOKOLER STEINER
Los Angeles, California

LIKE A GRANDMOTHER

I never really knew my grandparents. My Grandma Lynette, the only grandparent alive when I was born, died when I was only four. My family has a canon of hilarious stories about Lynette, an intensely opinionated woman with four former husbands. But my foggy memories of her are merely the minty taste of Kellogg's Grasshopper mint cookies (always stocked in a plastic jar on her counter), a glass cat statue with one missing beaded eye that held her bedroom door open, and the chunky jewelry around her neck, which now clutters my own mother's drawer.

And so, instead of biological grandparents of my own, I had Margaret Garten.

"Margie" was an older woman from a coal-mining town in West Virginia, with a twangy accent and a genius for cooking up pots of hot, thick chicken and dumplings. She was my babysitter (and full-on grandmother) throughout my childhood. She had escaped an abusive husband and fled to Chicago after raising her children. Babysitting the local children of our North Side neighborhood was both a supplementary income, and a way for her to connect with young families in our area. Her apartment was about a block away, and everyone in the vicinity knew of her. We had Halloween parties at her house, and craft days, and homework-helping study sessions. She never even finished grade school, but my dad said she was the wisest person he knew.

Margie's place in my life gave me a taste of just how special the relationship between children and grandparents (whether biological or not) can be.

ANNA J. WILLIAMS (22)
Chicago, Illinois

IN THE SHADE OF DADAJI'S TREE

"Dr. Chinta Haran Prasad's mango tree," everyone called it. Majestic, commanding and generous to all, my grandfather's tree—like the man himself—had a lofty reputation throughout Patna, the ancient, mystical Indian city on the southern banks of the river Ganges. For me, both of them were special friends in a strange and sometimes lonely ancestral home.

In the late 1950s, my grandfather spent several years in London acquiring a medical degree, and upon returning to Patna, his gift to his waiting wife and six young children was a beautiful old mansion surrounded by a large meadow and innumerable trees. My father, their youngest, was just a year old.

By the time I was born in that house in 1990, my grandmother was long gone. Dadaji was fighting a serious illness and only a few years from being permanently bedridden. And yet he remained a revered personage in Patna. I can still recall his lean frame walking slowly along the driveway, pausing playfully to chide three-year-old me. *"Deviji!"* ("Goddess") he would call me, and earn my giggly response. He might have once been an intimidating master of the house to his children, but I perceived him as my tender companion. He remains the most charming man I have ever encountered in my life—modern in his thoughts, humble in his ways. Even at age seventy, he had not let time tarnish his vogue.

I remember lying under the tree and admiring its long branches, strong and powerful as I pictured Dadaji in his prime. Its thick leaves, heavy with fruit, cast such dark shade, you almost felt as though it was night whenever you stretched out beneath them. Its brunette trunk, the green meadow, the burgundy brick walls of the mansion, were all the perfect recipe for an artist's canvas. Although I actually only lived there for a portion of my early childhood, much of which I barely remember, I developed a profound attachment to the house I was born in. I couldn't help but feel that this, more than any other place, was home.

When Dadaji passed away, I was still a very young child and barely understood the meaning of death. At his funeral, I obediently folded my hands in prayer and watched my parents' tear-stained faces through the corners of my eyes. I did not cry, but I knew that something was permanently changed. On sultry evenings, my cousin and I would sit on the terrace of the mansion, gazing at the darkening skies. She would point at the circular clouds and tell me they were Dadaji's spectacles, and that he was looking down and smiling at us. I chose to believe it.

Four years later we moved to Mumbai and I went off to boarding school. Dadaji's six offspring had all spread their wings and there was no one left to look after the house. The beautiful place I had once called home became a crumbling object of neglect.

But in my mind's eye, it remained magical: playing with my rambunctious dogs in the winter sun and showing them off to our wary neighbors, transforming the mango into an opulent tree house for my cousin's wedding, sneaking into Dadaji's office to inspect his clacking typewriter, his important files, his mysterious medicines. As time passed, and I moved to New York to attend university, the memories only grew stronger.

Last year, for the first time in more than a decade, I returned to Patna. The mansion has been divided into multiple dwellings and somehow is still known by our family name. The tenants are longtime townspeople, older folks who warmly remember Dadaji. They remembered me too and exclaimed over how much I had grown, and eagerly demanded stories of America. The meadow where generations once played and dreamed is gone; a metro-style apartment house stands in its place. The majestic tree that represented my childhood, and the untold stories of many before me, is no more. All who recall it—far-flung family members on a visit, old neighbors who still live nearby—grow reminiscing eyes as they gaze upon the empty space where it once reigned and its fragrant fruits ripened.

There is no proof that Dr. Chinta Haran Prasad's mango tree ever existed. How I wish there was something tangible left of it for me to hold onto. But now and then, wherever in the world I may be, I gaze up at the sky and see a face in the puffy clouds—bespectacled eyes smiling warmly at me, approving of the woman I've become. And that becomes enough.

ADYA SINHA (23)
Patna, India, and New York

Journaling Expedition #1

The Stories We Tell

What are three things I hope my grandchildren will tell their children about me someday?

1. _____
_____
_____

_____

_____

2. _____

_____

_____

_____

_____

3. _____

_____

_____

_____

_____

What are three things I could possibly start doing, or could do more of, or do better, to become the person I want to be in their eyes?

1. _____

_____

_____

_____

_____

2. _____

_____

_____

_____

_____

3. _____

_____

_____

_____

_____

CHAPTER II

IDENTIFYING YOUR FAMILY'S CORE VALUES: WORKBOOK FOR A GRAND NEW VISION

"Over fifty years ago, before this couple was even married, they would sit on the porch, look up at the stars and think about their future together... In their minds they could see their future children – they talked about the way they would raise them and what they wanted them to be like when they grew up... She would then go in the house and write down all the dreams and ideas they had talked about... Fifty years later, she still had what she wrote saved in her cedar chest... each year on their anniversary, they would read them as a family. They would ask the children if they wanted to add anything... and then she'd write their thoughts down. The children took copies with them when they married. She said: 'Everything we wrote has come true for ourselves and for our three children.'"

—Stephen R. Covey, *How to Develop a Family Mission Statement* (Audio CD)

In chapter 1, I examined some milestones of my own grandparenting journey—its twists and turns, challenges and rewards.

Now it's your turn.

As a new or first-time grandparent, you're in good company. At the time I'm writing this (according to the 2011 MetLife Report on American Grandparents), one in four American adults is a grandparent; by the year 2020, that number will rise to one in three—or 65 million Americans.

No doubt you're thrilled to be called Grandma or Grandpa, Nani or Poppie, Bubbie or Zaydie (or, like one spry duo of my acquaintance, "Bubbles and Zany"). At the same time, it may still come as a bit of a shock. Just yesterday, you were pushing your own babies in their strollers, and now those babies are having babies. Clichés like "it all goes by, before you know it!" turn out to be absolutely true.

What no longer rings true, however, is the classic image of America's grandparents as depicted in the Norman Rockwell-style tableaux: white-haired white folks wiling away their days in their front-porch rockers, waiting for all the kids and grandkids to converge after church for a home-cooked Sunday supper.

Your Generation

It's possible that this stereotype never fit your family of origin to begin with, as it contains few of the flavors found in the stewpot of 21st-century America. Or maybe it describes your own grandparents right down to their steel-rimmed bifocals and walking sticks. Except—they were so *OLD!* You may be (like I once was) a grandparent barely into your fifties, or even younger—still in the workforce, running half-marathons, with other children, teenagers, still living at home. Or even if you are a senior citizen, you're much too active and attractive to think of yourself that way.

If so, you're one of the lucky ones. Plenty of older adults don't feel very spry at all; taking grandchildren to Disneyworld isn't in the realm of possibility. Regardless of chronological age, no one is immune from chronic illness or worsening disability, financial downturns, caregiving responsibilities, or other harsh realities.

Notwithstanding your circumstances, or what "the other grandparents" can do, you have priceless gifts to bestow upon the grandchildren who look up to you, whether you're sharing a rafting trip down the Colorado River or a Hershey bar at your kitchen table.

That is the essence and the beauty of this singular relationship, whose sweetness will brighten your days.

One thing for sure: wherever you fit in the pantheon of contemporary grandparents, the very definition of what an American family looks like has changed dramatically from what it was even 25 years ago. While much of it's for the better, the wheels of change are turning more rapidly than we could have anticipated, and we are all holding on for the ride.

The stabilizing force of extended family — for *every kind of family* — is more important than ever.

*Who Are You and **Your** Family?*

So what are your fondest hopes and dreams for the family you've created, in the years that lie ahead? What can you do, in practical terms, to align yourself, your children, and their children in a close and mutually supportive relationship? It's an enormously challenging question when we're likely talking about **a highly diverse group of gloriously idiosyncratic individuals**, all of them in very different places in their lives — personally, professionally, economically, and geographically.

Like all journeys, it begins with the proverbial single step. And that step is **defining who you are as individuals and as a collective.** Going forward, this chapter, primarily a workbook, will give you some ideas of how to do just that through a trifecta of family-based initiatives that will pay big dividends:

- **Initiative #1: FAMILY MEETINGS** in which everyone takes turns being a teacher and learner;
- **Initiative #2: FAMILY VISION QUIZ**—an excellent addendum to a Family Meeting agenda (especially if it's your first such meeting!) to help identify your core values and interests;
- **Initiative #3: FAMILY VISION STATEMENT** that expresses who you are and aspire to be as a family and that can serve as a basis for shared activities in which everyone is a stakeholder.

Benefits of Journaling

For the very best shot at actually achieving your Family Vision, take a cue from the long-married couple that Stephen Covey described so charmingly in the quote at the beginning of this chapter.

- **Put it in writing**.

Over the course of fifty-plus years as a social-work professional and mentor, I've discovered that a simple pen or pencil can be one of the most successful tools to inspire self-discovery, lasting growth, and life satisfaction.

In an online article titled "The Health Benefits of Journaling," social-work professional Maud Purcell states: "The act of writing accesses your left brain, which is analytical and rational. While your left brain is occupied, your right brain is free to create, intuit and feel. In sum, writing removes mental blocks and allows you to use all of your brainpower to better understand yourself, others and the world around you." (*http://psychcentral.com/lib/2006/the-health-benefits-of-journaling/*)

My own experience strongly corroborates Ms. Purcell's assertions, as does a wealth of literature in the field. It is universally acknowledged that journaling can help you to:

- **"Know Thyself."** Addressing the past, present, and future in writing heightens our awareness of the forces that shape us. Making a conscious effort to understand ourselves is essential if we hope to understand our relationships.

- **Appreciate.** Sometimes all we need in order to value the good stuff in our lives and families is to see it in black and white. The simple act of appreciating can confer a huge boost of optimism and energy—and that stuff's contagious.

- **Address.** A family balance-sheet can also propel us to confront unpleasant issues that need addressing and old wounds that may still fester. This can spur on a key step in the journey toward healthy family relationships: the hugely liberating acts of trust-building and forgiveness (chapter 3).

- **Clarify** (and even problem-solve). Writing about ongoing conflicts (chapter 4), instead of seething or arguing over them, may help you sort out the details, put them in perspective, and understand another's point of view. This can actually help you resolve differences. Plus, when issues are on paper, nobody needs to rely on memory.

- **Decompress.** Getting things on paper can help get them out of your system, siphoning off anger and stress. In this way, journaling can be good for your blood pressure, your blood sugar, your sleep cycle, your heart, and your soul.

- **See the journey.** Journals can bring memories into sharp focus. Revisiting struggles and triumphs graphically illustrates how far you've come, which can empower you to keep TRYING and to keep growing.

- **Define and refine goals.** The Family Vision Statement that emerges from these exercises can become a springboard for shared adventures in good times, and for having a support system in place when you need it in hard times.

In Person and Unplugged

I've extolled the pen and pencil, but what about the use of laptops or iPads during Family Meetings? I say: go with what works, whatever is more conducive to individual family members' self-expression. Clearly, typing like the wind has become second nature to most, nowadays. But there's always the risk that kids (and adults) positioned behind computer screens will succumb to the lure of email or Facebook. And interestingly, a growing body of research ("How Handwriting Trains the Brain," *Wall Street Journal,* Oct. 5, 2010) reveals that the neurological and physical processes involved in writing *by hand* make it a more effective tool for learning and for imprinting memories than typing on a keyboard!

Think about it: Family Meetings might be the perfect opportunity for all three generations to spend some all-too-rare time together, unplugged. That's right: no cell phones either. Because everything (and everybody) you need, you already have, right there with you. So take a long moment to look around at each other and to quietly give thanks.

INITIATIVE #1: THE THREE-GENERATION FAMILY MEETING

Even if you raised your own kids having regular Family Meetings, the *three-generation* model—like all triangular human interactions—comes with its own set of complications and rewards.

Here's what Family Meetings should **never** be: forums for hashing out vendettas or for calling anybody onto the carpet. As Ellen, my daughter, observed: "Both my brother and I have worked hard in Family Meetings to keep the focus on family strengths, and on the strengths of each member. I've learned from management philosophy, and from my background in family/human development, that people are who they are. For me, the goal for with our family is to celebrate and build on strengths. We don't operate on a deficit model—i.e., what's broken and what do we have to fix. That's the job of family therapy."

Rules of Order

The first step is to create some basic rules of order to ensure that Family Meetings are built on a foundation of trust, civility, and respect, enabling communication to flourish. They can be read aloud at the beginning of each meeting. Here are some suggestions that have worked for our family:

- *Each of us will get opportunities to be the Teacher and the Learner, the Speaker and the Listener. We take turns and avoid interrupting each other.*

- *We don't put down others' ideas; we listen respectfully even when we disagree, striving to remain open-minded and not judgmental.*

- *We don't take it as a personal insult if someone does not share our opinions or beliefs.*

- *We strive to keep our tone gracious and our words kind. We don't yell, fight, ridicule, accuse, shame, or name-call.*

- *We hold uppermost in our minds that we've chosen to undertake this effort because we love and support each other.*

Here, again, I'll uphold the value of **TRYING.** Maybe you can't make *every* initiative in this workbook chapter get off the ground; maybe you won't get everybody's buy-in, every time. Whatever you *do* accomplish, however, will be a big step in the direction of a more enriching family connection.

Ten Tips for Great Family Meetings

There are many excellent resources, online and at your public library, for conducting Family Meetings; and all can be adapted to fit your needs and circumstances.

- *Institute meetings at regularly scheduled intervals that work for your family.* We email ahead to confirm meeting times during the holiday periods when we typically get together, which is once or twice a year, since we don't live near one another. Encourage commitment by keeping them a high priority. Begin and end on time.

- *Keep things focused with an agenda.* This too can be emailed ahead of time, with input from family members. Minutes that are taken and journaling exercises can become a family journal to look back on. The roles of leader and secretary can be rotated until everyone feels at ease with how to conduct an effective Family Meeting and depending on the teaching and learning to be done during that meeting.

- *Use "I-Messages."* This is a way of airing issues constructively that does not make others feel attacked or defensive. Example: instead of saying, "You always interrupt me and dominate the conversation!" say, "I feel badly when I'm interrupted. It makes me feel like my ideas don't matter."

- *Make sure that everyone feels heard.* If someone hasn't talked, ask, "What do you think?" If someone talks too much, stay respectful. You could say, "It sounds like this is important to you. We need to hear how everybody else feels about it." If someone is not showing respect, use an I-Message: "When I hear name-calling, I get concerned that we won't be able to cooperate."

- *Make decisions by consensus.* "Consensus" means communicating, problem-solving, and negotiating on major issues until no family member has any major objections to the decision—all can live with it. Decision-making by consensus incorporates the major needs and wants of all, in contrast with autocratic decision-making (which allows one person to decide) and democratic decision-making (which allows the majority to decide).

- *Summarize discussions/agreements to make sure you've actually achieved consensus.* Help clarify the proceedings with statements like "What I'm hearing us say we can all agree to do is . . ." or "Does anyone have any major objections to . . ." Look for nonverbal as well as verbal signs that a family member is uncomfortable with something.

- *If things get "too hot to handle," anyone can call for a break.* Take 15 minutes or whatever seems right before reconvening.

- *End with something fun that affirms good feelings.* Enjoy a family tradition—eat dessert, play a board game that everybody enjoys, watch a DVD together.

- *Debrief.* If you can't do it in writing by the end of the meeting, do it soon after, via email. Be attentive to what worked and what didn't.

- *Stay flexible and do what works.* As family members grow and change over time, so do rules for Family Meetings. If your family just cannot seem to find a time when everybody can get together, consider alternatives. Perhaps you can touch base with them individually on how they are doing.

Adapted from R. J. Fetch and B. Jacobson's fact sheet, "10 Tips for Successful Family Meetings" (4/07).
http://www.ext.colostate.edu/pubs/consumer/10249.html;
and Don Dinkelmyer, Jr.'s "Step Into Parenting,"
http://www.steppublsihers.com

INITIATIVE #2: A FAMILY VALUES QUIZ

A terrific agenda for your inaugural Family Meeting could include this short, stimulating quiz.

It may be tempting, initially, to try and define your family ethos by zeroing in on *shared interests*. But interests, hobbies, and activities, for a host of reasons, may wax and wane through the years. **Core values, however, tend to endure; and they are frequently the foundation for our lasting passions and enthusiasms.** A family with a core value of "outdoor adventures and fitness," for example, may relish taking ski trips together each winter. But what happens during years when money is tight or when a good portion of the family's members are either too old or too young to participate? Everyone can still have fun together and fulfill the same core value by going (or watching!) sledding or ice-skating in a local park.

By exploring and coming to terms with our family's areas of commonality and separateness, we teach the youngest generation how people of different beliefs respect each other, value each other's contributions, and manage to get along in the world.

Have fun taking the quiz, tallying the results, and discussing them. What will emerge is a kind of treasure map for your family life—a picture of the many rich attributes and values, interests, and convictions that each of you contributes to the collective, to make it a vibrant whole.

Be Flexible, Be Realistic

If you manage to distribute the Values Quiz at a Family Meeting or other gathering so that the entire clan—a captive, well-fed audience—can actually work on it together . . . congratulations!

For quite a few families, being in the same place at the same time just isn't feasible. This needn't deter you, however, from pursuing the objectives of this chapter.

You can get the ball rolling via email, forwarding materials to family members a month or more before a planned get-together, and asking them to send their responses back to you at least a week ahead of time. Then you or another family member who is adept at tabulating results (a middle-schooler, no doubt!) can aggregate the information ahead of time, ranking the different values based on which ones got the strongest responses from the most people. The journaling follow-up can be copied and pasted into a single document or spreadsheet.

If there's no family gathering on the horizon, or certain family members cannot attend, communications can take place via email or Skype, as long as you are willing (or someone else volunteers) to take on the position of secretary.

You may ask: but what if not everybody responds? Or if most respondents dash off one hasty reply to a journaling prompt, instead of a batch of thoughtful ones?

My answer: you TRIED, and you will still be ahead of where you were before. You'll have a picture, on paper, of your family's strongest shared values, favorite memories and activities, an excellent jumping-off point for discussion and action. Repeating this exercise every three to four years is another way to see where you have been and where you are going, as the generational wheel steadily turns.

OUR VALUES QUIZ

Value Description	Not Important	Somewhat Important	Very Important
Adventure (new experiences, challenge, excitement)			
Balance (appropriate attention devoted to various aspects of life and activities)			
Contribution and Generosity (desire to make a difference, to give)			
Cooperation (teamwork, working with others)			
Creativity and Artistic Expression (new ideas, innovation, experimenting, drama, painting, literature)			
Economic Security (freedom from financial worries)			
Fairness (equal chance, equal hearing for all)			
Family Happiness (desire to get along, respect, harmony)			
Friendship (intimacy, caring, support)			
Independence (self-reliance, freedom from controls)			

Value Description	Not Important	Somewhat Important	Very Important
Inner Harmony (desire to be at peace with oneself)			
Integrity (honesty, sincerity, consistent demonstration of your values)			
Learning (growth, knowledge, understanding)			
Personal Development (improvement, reach potential, excellence, high standards, minimal errors)			
Pleasure (enjoyment, fun, happiness)			
Spirituality (belief or interest in a higher power or God)			
Wisdom (desire to understand life, to exercise sound judgment)			
Interdependence (ability to ask for help and give help)			
Other *(fill in your choice)*			
Other			
Other			

INITIATIVE #3: CRAFTING A FAMILY VISION STATEMENT

Now that you've zeroed in on your values, you're ready to create a Vision Statement. (You read our family's Vision Statement in chapter 1.) Interestingly, delving into values often helps people discover **unexpected areas of commonality, notwithstanding what may appear to be striking differences of opinion.** Some families, for example, are very much split along political or ideological lines. There's nothing wrong with healthy disagreement and debate, of course; it's all part of a vibrant Teaching-and-Learning culture. But if, for example, social justice emerges as a strong core value for all or most family members, there are ways to *share* and *live* this that are decidedly nonpartisan. Families across the political spectrum, or with different religious beliefs or practices, can volunteer together in a soup kitchen or community renewal project and share articles or books that inspire them.

In an online article in *Psychology Today,* corporate strategist Jennell Evans defines vision statements in organizational terms that are easily adaptable to our family organizations:

An effective Vision Statement:

- defines the optimal desired future state—the mental picture—of what an organization wants to achieve over time;

- provides guidance and inspiration as to what an organization is focused on achieving in five, ten, or more years;

- functions as the "North Star"—it is what all stakeholders understand their work every day ultimately contributes toward accomplishing over the long term; and

- is written succinctly in an inspirational manner that makes it easy for all stakeholders to repeat it at any given time.

(http://www.psychologytoday.com/blog/smartwork/201004/
vision-and-mission-whats-the-difference-and-why-does-it-matter)

The "Three-Pronged" Statement

A popular format for characterizing your family's vision (or mission or ethos) is the three-pronged statement. Here's the template, courtesy of the website "Families with Purpose":

> **"TO** *(do something)* . . .
> **IN SUCH A WAY THAT** *(quality of action)* . . .
> **SO THAT** *(we gain these results or benefits)."*

Polly Schlafhauser, founder and president of Families with Purpose (an online resource for parents seeking to create "an authentic family life for themselves and their children"), characterized her own family's strong ethos via a three-pronged statement on the organization's website:

"TO *realize our dreams, goals, and aspirations as a family and as individuals* . . . IN SUCH A WAY THAT *stretches our intellect, enriches our Christian faith, strengthens our character, and enriches our family life* . . . SO THAT *we are fulfilled, happy, confident, and always close."*

To assist other families seeking to craft their own statements, Schlafhauser deconstructed the statement's three parts:

"TO" . . . **is where you declare the action.** What specific steps or actions are you going to take? What are the specific efforts you are going to make as a family? In our example, the action is "to realize our dreams, goals, and aspirations as a family and as individuals." Others may be "to communicate more effectively" or "to learn new things and new cultures."

"IN SUCH A WAY THAT" . . . **represents the quality of your action.** In what manner are you going to accomplish it? In a way that gets you what you want no matter what and in the fastest way possible, or one that nurtures your spirit, lets you be creative, grow individually and together? Our statement ensures that every action we take to "realize our dreams and goals" is going to be done in a manner that allows us to learn new things, deepens our faith, makes our family life better, and makes us better people.

"SO THAT" . . . is where you capture the results of your actions. What do you want to come out of all of this? Strong, independent kids? Successful and happy adults? Closer relationships? The priorities here are to be "fulfilled, happy, confident, and always close." ©2013 Families with Purpose LLC (with permission)
(http://www.familieswithpurpose.com/family-mission-statement.html)

Another Approach to Vision Statements

You may not wish to confine yourself to the three-pronged template. On her website, The Relationship Resource, blogger Amy Marshall, RN, expressed her family's vision this way:

> *"We are a family who believes that relationships matter most! We value spending time together and we endeavor to be the primary caregivers of our children. We hold each member of our family accountable for responsible behavior. We support each other in our individual pursuits of personal and professional interests. We cheer each other on. We laugh whenever possible. We hold our marital relationship as a top priority because this relationship serves as the foundation of our family."*
> *(http://www.everythingmom.com/dynamics/the-family-vision-statement-a-solution-for-challenging-decisions. html?print=1&tmpl=component)*

Marshall pointed out that their Vision Statement has become "an ideal . . . to live up to," and even a problem solver:

For example, we often revisit the major financial decision, whether to buy a new vehicle or continue cramming into our old small sedan. After briefly fantasizing about all-wheel drive and enough trunk space for a stroller and the groceries, we remind ourselves that space is a luxury that our budget doesn't allow for right now given our decision to sacrifice my regular, dependable, work scenario for a stay-at-home parent scenario. Decisions have become simpler, easier to make, and more comfortable to accept as they have been created in the context of our Family Vision that was crafted in the interest of our authentic family ideals.

Your Family's Turn

As this chapter has shown, a Family Vision can be approached in many ways. It's just worth trying to *have* one to light your way.

Our Family Vision Statement
"TO_____ _____
IN SUCH A WAY THAT_____ _____
SO THAT_____ _____.""
Dated:_____

THE GRANDCHILDREN SPEAK

EULOGY FOR GRANDPA ERNIE, 2012

At my Grandpa Ernie's funeral, I shared some life lessons he taught me:

1. Speeches should be short and sweet.
2. "Take it easy."
3. Brag about your grandkids; they're special.
4. It's never too cold for ice cream.
5. Surround yourself with family and friends.
6. Arguing keeps your mind sharp.
7. The best initials = EF (We shared them.)
8. You always need pens, at least three.
9. "Be prepared." (He was an Eagle Scout.)
10. Grandparents and grandkids get along because they share a common enemy.
11. Enjoy life: you only get one.

EMILY FANWICK (16)
Wilton, Connecticut

PENS WITH HER NAME ON THEM

My grandmother and I were very close. I was the firstborn grandchild, and we always had a special relationship. She was my cultural arts director—we went annually to *The Nutcracker*, she took me to my first opera and many plays and museums (many things my mom did not enjoy). She took me on my first trip to Europe, and when she had her second colon cancer surgery I promised that when she got better I would take her to Paris—which we did.

She had pens made with her name on them and gave them to everyone she encountered—the maître d' at The Plaza, the saleswoman at Bergdorf's, etc. I do not have pens but always bake before I go to my corporate office and give little gift bags to workers at the garages I park in, to the security people in the buildings we frequent, and more. No doubt, this is due to my grandmother.

JENNIFER ZOREK-PRESSMAN (55)
Westport, Connecticut

A PRICELESS SMILE

I found the following essay in August 2003, while cleaning out my grandmother's apartment in Florida after she passed away at the age of 93. I had attached a note saying: "Dear Grandma, I wrote this for my camp application in response to the question: 'Who is your hero and why?' I thought you might like a copy. I love you very, very much. Love, Alysa." The note was written in 1992, when I was twenty years old.

"Enjoy life, it is as easy as a positive attitude." Ask my grandmother for advice and she would tell you just that. Many years of life experience and my grandmother's eyes reflect that youth is a way of thinking, a mentality and not a measure of years. My grandmother is my inspiration and that is why she is also my hero. Have you heard of the phrase "smile and the world smiles with you"? Well, the world smiles with my grandmother. Watching her in action I have learned invaluable lessons I will carry on with me to live by and teach my grandchildren someday.

My grandma always reminds me, "It is just as easy to be nice as it is to be mean." She taught me not to pass judgment on someone else because there is usually more going on inside than meets the eye. My grandma is a firm believer in the compliment. Like smiles, they go a long way and are not just free—they are priceless. Feeling good about oneself is the inner glow each one of us needs to survive. Compliments are easy to give and their impact is without bounds. My grandma has definitely caught on to a good thing, I think I have too.

I still miss her every day as I try to live by her wisdom and by the love she left me as her lasting legacy.

RABBI ALYSA MENDELSON GRAF (41)
Westport, Connecticut

STRENGTH FROM THEIR EXAMPLE

One story (out of many), that gives me particular strength and courage: my grandfather happened to be traveling away from my grandmother and their two young boys when WWII started. The ports were closed and they lost communication with one another. They stayed true to one another and carried on with hope for years before they were reunited again. When I think of that, all my day-to-day challenges seem quite insignificant.

ANA CHARALAMBIDES (24)
Hartford, Connecticut

BROWNIES AND LOVE

I have learned so many things from my grandparents that I don't know where to begin. I'll be gentlemanly and start with Grandma, who is always joyful. Even when she is presented with the most difficult challenges life can offer, she takes everything in stride, and continues to smile, and laugh, and to handle the problem magnificently. Plus: she is singlehandedly responsible for my sweet tooth. My mouth waters at the very thought of her delicious banana bread and brownies. She spoils me—and I love it.

When I think of my grandfather, I think of the stoic businessman who taught me about the value of hard work and loyalty. Though he grew up with very little, Grandpa rose to become one of the top executives at Sears, through hard work. And loyalty? You'll never hear the end of how he was a Sears man, and to this day he continues to meet with his closest friends and associates for weekly brunches. On a more comical note, Grandpa has certainly taught me patience. One needs a great deal of patience when attempting to teach a senior citizen how to use all these blasted new technologies, like computers.

Most of all, my grandparents give me hope that love can endure in a world where this doesn't happen so easily. At my age, as I start to think about the idea of marriage, I sometimes wonder, "What's the point?" But I look at them, and I marvel at how they have persevered through all the ups and downs—growing stronger as a couple by facing everything together.

These musings hardly scratch the surface of all I have learned from them, and how much I treasure them.

MARC CORNFIELD (23)
Deerfield, Illinois

AN EDUCATED, SELF-SUFFICIENT WOMAN

Upon their marriage in 1946, my parents left their respective hometowns to move to Chicago, where my father had a job offer from a law firm. My grandfathers both died when I was about ten. Mom's mother visited (from far-off Cleveland, Ohio) only once a year, at Christmas. So Grandmommy McMillen, from downstate Decatur, Illinois, was the one grandparent I got to know, and mostly as a widow, still living in the Victorian-style house where she'd raised my father, just a few blocks from her own childhood home. During my visits to her house, and her visits to my childhood home in suburban Chicago, she became a role model for me, both in her affectionate good humor and in the multifaceted intellectual accomplishments which ranged from running her inherited corn and cattle farm outside Decatur, to traveling throughout Europe. Through my grandmother I glimpsed a future for myself as an educated, self-sufficient woman.

PATRICIA R. McMILLEN (60)
Oak Park, Illinois

Journaling Expedition #2

After the Meeting

Here are some debriefing questions we've found helpful. You can photocopy the following worksheet—or one like it that better suits your needs—and hand it out after each meeting. Or debrief more informally, if that's what everyone prefers.

Debriefing Journal: Our Family Meeting

What are the main things you believe we accomplished at today's meeting?

- _____
- _____
- _____
- _____

What did you enjoy most about today's meeting, and why?

- _____
- _____
- _____
- _____

What would you like to see on the agenda for our next meeting?

- _____
- _____
- _____
- _____

What aspect(s) did you enjoy least, and why?

- _____
- _____
- _____
- _____

Do you propose any changes to the overall structure of our Family Meeting? (Too long/too short, more often/less, etc.?)

- _____
- _____
- _____
- _____

Debriefing Journal: Our Family Values Quiz

What are your first impressions of your values quiz results? Is the picture it paints what you expected, or are there surprises?

Do the results please you, or do you wish they were different in any way? What do you see as the most valuable insight of this exercise?

_____

_____

_____

_____

What are the three most important values, for you personally? Can you rank them, and share why they resonate for you so strongly? Is there a story that goes with your deep attachment?

_____

_____

_____

_____

Do any activities or family initiatives immediately come to mind, that you like to see as an outgrowth of this exercise? You can group these into those that are fairly easily attained, like "we start a family book club," to more complicated undertakings that are farther in the future and would require more planning (i.e., "We take a family 'roots' trip to Ireland, together"). *Note: later on, you can elaborate on one or more of these initiatives and begin planning in earnest, in your "Let's Go and Do" wish-list at the end of chapter 7.*

_____

_____

_____

_____

CHAPTER III

GATEWAY TO THE GRANDEST LOVE: REBUILDING TRUST, ACHIEVING FORGIVENESS

"Be slow to anger, quick to forgive."
—Ethics of the Fathers

"What can you do to promote world peace?
Go home and love your family."
—Mother Teresa

The Promise of a New Life

By the time we reach the grandparenting stage, we've all endured some of life's unforeseeable twists and turns—tragedy, disappointment, loss. And then along comes this brand-new bud on the family tree. Even the most disaffected soul can feel the unabashed stirrings of a poet: a new leaf, a new dawn—purity and innocence, sweetness and light.

"A baby is nature's way of giving the world another chance." It's an uplifting quote everyone's heard in one form or another. And never is it more true than when that baby is your own grandchild.

Grandparenting can provide a renewed sense of wonder and purpose for us as older adults and a rekindling of memories. Memories of our own children's early years—inhaling the scent of a newborn, pushing a little one *"higher, higher!"* on a swing, taking them to their first movie. Even memories of our own childhoods, and our own parents and grandparents, so long ago.

Nothing can turn back the clock, but as grandparents, we're able to revel in that rarest of gifts: a second chance, a chance to be and do better this time, to make old wrongs right; a chance to smooth over bad feelings. (And which family doesn't have some of those?)

But second chances aren't always offered automatically. Often they require us to take an honest look at the past and figure out how it might stand in the way of fulfilling family relationships in the present and future—and then try to do something about it. And that's what this chapter is all about.

Relationships with Adult Children

Grandparents, it comes down to this: our adult offspring are the gatekeepers to The Grandest Love. If there is too much unfinished business or lingering hurt, we don't simply get to leapfrog over the unpleasantness and blithely take our do-over with the next generation. In certain aspects, grandparenting presents an opportunity to be a more engaged, impactful, loving family member than you may have been capable of being two or three decades ago. But it's not a *parenting* do-over that wipes your slate clean.

You are not your grandchild's parent. Nor are you your adult child's full-fledged partner in raising the next generation, except in those circumstances where this is, in fact, the case (i.e., situations in which grandparents share or obtain custody of their grandchildren).

The Grandest Love is a new ballgame with new rules and new roles. Before you can embrace those roles to the fullest, however, there is often healing work to do within your family: acknowledging past hurts and missteps, rebuilding trust, seeking and offering forgiveness—with your adult children, primarily, but often also with their spouses, significant others, and even in-laws.

A Chance to Make Things Better

The good news is the arrival of a new grandchild opens an ideal window of opportunity for doing that healing work. After all, you and your adult offspring have something new and extraordinary in common: **you're both parents now.** Presumably, they're flooded with overwhelming awe and love for the new life they've been called upon to nurture and protect—and an overwhelming uncertainty, too, as they worry about whether they'll be equal to the task.

Welcome to our world, kids! Because isn't that just how we felt—and continue to feel—through every stage of parenting, and with each highly idiosyncratic offspring?

No question, there's truth to that insufferable mantra that's passed from generation to generation: "Someday, when YOU have kids, YOU'LL UNDERSTAND."

What will they understand? **That for the most part, we did the very best we knew how, under our circumstances at the time.**

Some offspring seem to get this *without* having to struggle through parenthood themselves. But for those who needed an extra jolt, the recognition of their own parents' humanness and best intentions may be so humbling that it unleashes a rush of warmth and gratitude. Jump on that and cultivate it with care, and all three generations will reap the benefits. In chapter 4 ("Reducing Conflict"), we'll talk about specific ways to do that.

Old Baggage, Simmering Resentments

In some instances, it will take more than shared delight over a new baby to wipe away years of contentiousness or resentment or to reopen lines of communication that have long been clogged.

The reality is, some stumbling blocks in our relationships with our adult children may be products of a past that is impossible to undo, or to redo: if you underwent an acrimonious divorce, for example, or were a workaholic when (they continue to insist) they needed you most. You may have been genuinely obligated to give your attention elsewhere—to an ill parent, to another child with special needs, to an organization or business that rested heavily on your shoulders—but the end result was your absence made a particular child feel undervalued.

Particularly if your children's teen years and early twenties were laden with conflict, the unhappy memories and recriminations can go both ways: the times you felt scared to death because they were acting out in ways that put them in harm's way; the times you felt wounded when they seemed to flout your most deeply held values. And their resentment over your miscalibrated responses—in coming down too hard on them, or not hard enough.

Even if it's all old baggage that's barely relevant anymore and the details have become hazy, you may still feel weighed down by it.

Long-past demons are bad enough. *Ongoing* conflicts, fed by a **wellspring of anger** that keeps replenishing itself, can be even more destructive. You may harbor a cauldron of resentments about their choice of life partner, their work, their religious or political attitudes, their sexual behavior, where they live, their friends, and so on. They may have their own simmering cauldron dedicated to your opposition and perceived judgmentalism, your laundry-list of old mistakes or behaviors they are less than fond of.

Cauldrons of resentment filled with toxic ingredients—like leftovers of a past that cannot be undone—do not bode well for an unfettered grandparenting relationship with the tiny, "innocent bystander" who has just burst upon the scene. In fact, sharply differing notions about Bringing Up Baby can provide you and your adult children with a whole new universe of issues upon which to disagree, adding *more* bitterness to the brew.

Forgiveness Is a Priority

If you're already living this way, you know how exhausting it is, how corrosive to relationships, body, and soul. A new grandchild—even if he or she is not your first—can be your chance to courageously lead your family forward on a better path, a path upon which you can teach your family members, through your words and deeds, how to eschew divisiveness and behave like peacemakers. A path where you can learn where you went wrong in the past and try to do better.

Instead of allowing anger to do its corrosive work in your family, how about actively seeking to harness the healing power of forgiveness? Says Katherine M. Piderman, Ph.D., staff chaplain at the Mayo Clinic:

> There's no one definition of forgiveness. But in general, forgiveness is a decision to let go of resentments and thoughts of revenge. Forgiveness is the act of untying yourself from thoughts and feelings that bind you to the offense committed against you. This can reduce the power these feelings otherwise have over you, so that you can live a freer and happier life in the present. Forgiveness can even lead to feelings of understanding, empathy and compassion for the one who hurt you.
>
> When you don't practice forgiveness, especially in your family relationships, you and your family—including children and grandchildren—may be the ones who pay most dearly. (http://evangelistdavidlight.webs.com/forgiveothersyes.htm)

Create a Family Culture of Forgiveness

As Dr. Piderman further points out, forgiveness—seeking it as well as offering it—is "a process," not a one-time thing. I believe that we as grandparents must plow fertile ground for this process by establishing **a culture of forgiveness** in our families. This means not only with our adult offspring but also with their spouses or significant others, if they're partnered; with the in-laws (the "other" grandparents); with ex-spouses who may be parents of our grandchildren; and with the grandchildren themselves, once they are old enough to grasp the concept.

What does it mean to promote a culture of forgiveness?

- **Not ignoring signs** that we may have hurt a family member and reaching out to them with concern and humility if we have.

- **Not masking** our own hurt feelings with aloof or angry behavior that is difficult for others to decipher and address.

- Striving to make **compassion our default mode** in how we view and interpret a family member's actions.

- Using **respectful language and a loving tone of voice** when we talk about what is bothering us.

- Regularly acknowledging that **being open to forgiveness— seeking it, offering it, promoting it—is a core value in our family.**

Forgiveness and reconciliation are core values of all the world's major religions and are a central attribute upheld by nonbelievers as well. For many years, I've embraced the Jewish tradition of phoning my family members, friends, and colleagues (of all backgrounds) around the fall High Holy Days, to wish everyone a good year ahead, to ask their forgiveness for anything I may have done to wrong them, and to offer my own reassurances to them. You certainly don't have to be Jewish or religious to undertake an annual commemoration of forgiveness! Examining your family's beliefs and expectations regarding forgiveness, and sharing stories that emphasize its value, can serve as an excellent agenda for a Family Meeting.

Forgiveness is a process that may take a very long time. But it too starts with that single step. Often that step is a candid conversation with a loved one, in which you say sincerely: "I'd like to talk about [an issue from the past], because I don't want it to get in the way of the way of our family's wonderful connection and feelings about the future."

"Separate Realities" of Parents and Children

San Francisco-based psychologist **Joshua Coleman, Ph.D.**, is the author of *When Parents Hurt: Compassionate Strategies When You and Your Grown Child Don't Get Along* (Harper Collins, 2008). In a blog post for UC Berkeley's Greater Good Science Center, Dr. Coleman recommends:

> *Honor the "separate realities" nature of family life. Just because you made decisions with your child's best interest in mind, doesn't mean that they were experienced in the way that you intended. Don't try to prove them wrong . . . Take responsibility for whatever mistakes you have made as a parent. If there's a kernel of truth to your child's complaint, speak to the kernel of truth.*
> *(http://greatergood.berkeley.edu)*

Let's face it: there are separate realities for parents and children in practically every family. Even those that are relatively minor and long past, have the power to destroy relationships when people don't acknowledge them and make amends. Take the case of Mrs. R., whose family saga is recounted here by her former neighbor. It's a worst-case scenario, to be sure. But sadly, don't almost all of us know—or know of—a Mrs. R.?

Unforgiven: One Family's Story

My former neighbor, Mrs. R., was a hardworking widow and a devoted mother. Helen, her older child, was a brilliant student; but there was no question that charming, easygoing Sammy was the apple of his mother's eye. She didn't think anybody was good enough for her son—not even Karen, the lovely young woman Sammy began dating when both were college freshmen. Still, Mrs. R. was livid when she learned that Karen had broken up with him.

Only a few months later, the young couple reunited. But Mrs. R. insisted she would have nothing to do with her son until he came to his senses and dumped the "no-good tramp" who had wounded him!

That was more than 25 years ago. Sammy and Karen are married parents of three—successful in their careers, active in their church and community.

Unbelievably, Mrs. R. kept her word. She never spoke to them again.

At first, Sammy and Karen tried to make peace. But after Mrs. R. refused invitations to their wedding, and their oldest child's baptism and birthday parties, their overtures ceased. They began bad-mouthing her as bitterly as she bad-mouthed them.

Their children were the only grandchildren Mrs. R. would ever have. She's in her late eighties now, in the final stages of Alzheimer's. Helen takes care of her, and the relations between the two siblings are extremely strained. Sammy's family feels no obligation to the bitter woman who they know only as a living symbol of what it means to hold a grudge.

Mrs. R.'s story taught me one of the most important lessons I'll ever learn. I remember vividly how her kids were everything to her, just like my recently-married daughter is to me! How could things go so terribly awry?

Everyone who hears this story says: "A bump in the road of a college romance—that's a ridiculous reason for a lifelong rift!" And they're right, of course. But when you think about it: what's a GOOD reason for anger and blame that does not recede?

I've promised myself I'll be proactive so that grudges never take root between my daughter, son-in-law and me. I will offer and seek forgiveness immediately whenever hurt feelings or misunderstandings arise (as they inevitably do). It's a tragic waste to do otherwise!

—Marta (48), New Jersey

Estrangement: A Tragic Scenario

Mrs. R.'s story is extreme, yes, but hardly unique. Estrangement between parents and one or more of their adult children may even be a "silent epidemic" in this country, according to a number of experts. If this story brought a tear to your eye, perhaps you are one of them.

Cornell University gerontologist Dr. Karl Pillemer interviewed approximately 1,500 individuals over the age of 65 for his book, *30 Lessons for Living: Tried and True Advice from the Wisest Americans* (Hudson Street Press, 2011). Here's what his research revealed about estrangement:

> Among the saddest people I met in interviews with older Americans . . . were those living in this situation. The destruction of the parent-child bond was a persistent source of melancholy, a feeling of incompleteness that weighed down the soul. And the one failed relationship is not necessarily mitigated by having warm, fulfilling ties with other offspring. Almost all of the elders who found themselves with one child who was lost to them or with whom there was bad blood felt unresolved or incomplete. Such feelings only became more acute as they neared the end of life. *(http://legacyproject.human.cornell.edu/2012/02/avoiding-and -healing-estrangement-from-a-child/)*

"Particularly acute," writes Dr. Pillemer, "is the separation from grandchildren that can occur as a result of the rift."

Indeed, some of the most heartbreaking stories I've ever been privy to are those of grandparents who have been barred from contact with their grandchildren in the wake of an adult child's divorce or custody battle—in some instances, grandchildren they previously may have been supporting or even raising. **With a divorce rate hovering around 50% and the marked increase in the number of couples who have children together outside of marriage, few grandparents today can say**

with assurance that their own families will remain forever immune.

In chapter 10, I've listed a number of resources for grandparents struggling with estrangement and other "tough stuff" scenarios. On these pages, we'll focus on *prevention* of family rifts and early intervention through seeking and offering forgiveness.

We Take the Lead in Rift Prevention

Cornell's Dr. Pillemer offers some practical advice on how to defuse conflicts that may lead to serious rifts:

- **See the potential rift early and defuse it.** *The elders acknowledge that once the rift sets in, it takes on a life of its own and becomes much more difficult to repair. The time to act is when the first warning signs show themselves. Martha, 74, who had a major blow-up with her son and daughter-in-law, said: "I should never have let things deteriorate the way they did. Looking back, I could see problems brewing and I couldn't hold back from criticizing my daughter-in-law." Parents of adult sons and daughters need to ask themselves: Is the battle worth it? The elders told me that usually it's not.*

- **Act immediately after the rift occurs.** *The elders warn that the viewpoints of both parties harden quickly; in a relatively short time, it becomes easier not to make the effort to reconcile than to try to do so. The new reality sets in fast; therefore, the time to "make things better" is as soon as possible after the blow-up. Janice, 72, spoke about her problems with her daughter, Gloria: "After our big fight, I should have had a heart-to-heart with Gloria right away. After a week or two, we were both so angry—and I guess hardened—that it was terribly difficult even to start a conversation." In contrast, Maria, 82, was very disappointed and angry at her son, because he would not help Maria care for his father during his last illness. But she decided to act as soon as possible. She sat down with him and told him exactly how she felt, allowing a reconciliation to take place. "It's worth it," she told me, "not to feel like I might lose what I have that's good with my son."*

- *It's often the parent who needs to compromise. I am well aware that this sounds unfair; however, in my review of the accounts of intergenerational rifts, it's usually the parent who pays the higher price if a rift occurs. Older mothers and fathers tend to invest more in the relationship as they get older and therefore stand to lose more by letting it disintegrate. Many elders recommended that parents try their best to "forgive the unforgivable." Some have had the worst happen, stood on the brink of the rift, and decided that it still wasn't worth the end of the relationship with the child.*

- *So here's a key life lesson from America's elders: avoid the rift. Of course, it is possible that a child's behavior is so damaging or dangerous for a parents' physical or mental health that separation is needed. But the elders tell us that rifts usually occur over less extreme matters that seem important at the time but are almost never worth the pain of separation when you reach your later years. (http://legacyproject.human.cornell. edu/2012/02/avoiding-and-healing-estrangement-from-a-child/) (With permission)*

Finally, all the experts recommend: **patience.** Relationships don't become tense overnight, and the tensions don't defuse overnight either. In the best-case scenario, your adult child will echo your sincere wish for a flourishing relationship and will eagerly look to you as a hands-on grandparent. Or you may need to reach out for a while. Don't give up. The universe has given you a second chance, with that new bud on your family tree. There's no greater joy than watching it blossom and no greater satisfaction than helping it along.

How do you want to tell the story of your life? If you run into an old high school chum, someone you haven't seen in years, what would your story be? Are you holding on to a tale of bitter recriminations, an elaborate litany of how you were wronged?

If so, and if it's a tale you can't bring yourself to let go of, the rest of this book may not have much to offer you. Because it's about the joys—and challenges—of Teaching and Learning, giving and taking, sharing and doing. But without forgiving and making amends, you're not embracing that precious, miraculous second chance.

THE GRANDCHILDREN SPEAK

EVERY LIFE, A LESSON

My grandfather beat my grandmother. I don't know how many times—at least once, probably more. There are police photos, but I've never seen them. After they divorced, my grandma was left raising five kids on her own on Chicago's South Side. She was a divorced single mom in the 1950s with no skill set, no family support, and no money. She worked three jobs—crossing guard, waitress, whatever paid—while my grandfather refused to pay child support. He went to jail for that, I think. I don't know how many times, but at least once.

My grandfather also called me Jilly-bean, built me a backyard fort, married a wonderful single mother who I knew as one of my three grandmas, and was an involved father and grandfather to his second family. I adored him.

When he died, it was quick and painless—fine one day, gone the next. An entire busload of his friends came to the wake. Everyone remembered how he loved poker, how he loved to bake in the sun. Two young Marines folded a flag over his coffin at his Catholic funeral. His children and grandchildren spoke; we all cried.

My grandma died after a decade-long descent into dementia, a shell of her former self. She didn't remember taking me to pick Bachelor's Buttons from her garden, teaching me how to make necklaces out of clover, singing the songs she wrote about mama cats and their kittens to my sister and me. There was no funeral. We scattered her ashes across the Shenandoah Valley.

There are lessons in how they both lived—the importance of resilience, the necessity of self-reliance, the truth of real and transformative change. There are ripples they both left—generations of steely women, families that boomerang between enmity and forgiveness.

The lessons in how they died are less satisfying. In the end, a life of struggle undertaken by a woman who deserved better in every way—a life without security or money or physical safety, a life where work and misery were rewarded with flickers of light and beautiful moments—still ended unfairly. Ended with those moments erased from her memory. Ended with so much less than she deserved.

JILL FILIPOVIC (30)
Brooklyn, New York

THE QUARTET

Omama Gina, our dance was through a flicker of time. So out of place in 1950s Newark; plump, romantic, pre-Raphaelite sprite, with garlands in her hair. We sprawled on her living-room rug, drawing rainbows and sunbursts, princesses and unicorns. And oh we danced, channeling her rebellious sister, the one who had beguiled Kafka. Gina's (hard "G") wistful aquamarine gaze—was she always yearning? Was it for her girlhood in Poland, before blood coursed down the cobblestones of Tarnow? Or was she pining for a husband more gallant than the dour, withholding cantor?

She called me *Himmlisches Wesen* (Heavenly Creature), bathing me in the tenderness she never received, introducing me to art, to movement, to the poetry of the imagination. She was 59 and I was seven when she died, suddenly.

Opapa Juda, for you I felt mostly fear. He clung to the tenets of his faith more ardently and knew them better than he ever seemed to know or care for us. While Omama still lived, their apartment was welcoming, redolent of chicken soup; with him alone, it felt chilly and austere. I found its dark, heavy European furnishings inexplicably menacing. He once caught me defiling the Sabbath by writing and sketching when I thought he was napping. He seized my artwork and berated me with such ferocity that I refused to stay with him overnight ever again. Years later, long after he was gone, I realized that underneath his harshness, he too was yearning—for parents and siblings swallowed up in the Lodj Ghetto. I felt love for him only when my brother and I sat at his feet, on the *bimah* of his synagogue—where he loomed over us, over everyone, in a black satin robe and tall *chazzen's* hat, swaying, chanting, bursting forth with the liturgical melodies of Europe and the atonal wails of Israel. It was there, on that *bimah,* that he collapsed and died after trudging to shul one frigid Saturday morning. To my brother he bequeathed his gifts for music; I got only the love of it—but God, that was a lot.

Großvater Aaron, I never knew you. All I have of him is a charcoal portrait—rakish, broody, movie-star handsome—hanging in my foyer. His insistence that he would abandon his beloved Berlin *"nur mit dem letzen zug"* ("only on the last train") cost him his life; by the time he agreed to leave, Hitler had slammed shut the gate. My parents often reproached me for displaying Aaron Orbach's penchant for last-minute departures. I don't know what he would have been to me, in life. In death, he put a face on history and ignited my fervor for social justice.

Großmutter Nelly: living under our roof, you were the steadfast companion of my youth. My father swore, after Auschwitz, that he would never again be separated from her. Though her legs were failing (from a trolley accident for which she dared not seek medical attention, during the war), she and my father remained a formidable duo: ferociously smart, bawdy and combative. They invariably eclipsed my genteel, weary mother. That she spoke only German ensured I would grow up bilingual, because I— like she—hungered to know everything and would tolerate no secrets. Together we watched television nonstop: *The Price is Right, As the World Turns, The Donna Reed Show, Twilight Zone,* Yankee baseball, *Million Dollar Movie.* I was her translator, both of us seeking to comprehend and to mimic, through that glowing box in the darkened den, what it meant to be American.

It was fitting that after she departed, it was time for me to go too. She died weeks before my high-school graduation. Hungry to know and do everything, I left for New York and college at 16, and never looked back.

What remains most vivid, from all those years at home, is her nightly prayer. So many times I stood outside her bedroom door, listened to her breathe, and waited. She recited the words, always the identical words, in a strong, even voice:

"Lieber Gott, ich danke dir . . ."

"Dear God, I thank you . . . for all that I received, for all that I am now receiving, and for all that I have yet to receive."

Each time I heard it, I could scarcely wrap my head around it. With all that she—that our family—had endured . . . how could she still summon this naive gratitude?

Yet there it was.

Nellyschen, companion of my youth: your gratitude became mine. It defines me.

I am grateful for you—for all of you—and for everything you taught me; and especially grateful for your children (of blessed memory), my most loving parents.

VIVIEN ORBACH-SMITH
Wilton, Connecticut

ETHEL'S TALES

Every time I open a bottle of Veuve Clicquot, I think of my paternal grandmother not only because of her natural effervescence but because of her strong resemblance to Madame Clicquot, whose stoic image appears on the tiny metal cap above the cork.

Grandma Ethel also looked a little like George Washington. Unlike George, however, she didn't always tell the truth, but would instead embellish facts in such a clever, loving way as to steer the entire family into her way of thinking. For instance, Donald, the little boy who lived across the street from her, was never available for my cousin Pam and me to play with because, insisted Grandma, "He's in jail." (In fact, he was just a little too rough for her tastes.)

Ethel may have lived in Beverly Hills, but her protective instincts, especially where the children were concerned, hearkened back to her own childhood in Russia. "They wouldn't let us go to school," I can still hear her tell me, some 33 years after her death (peacefully, in her sleep, thank you very much). It was understood who "they" were, and her words echo in my head every time I witness any sort of discrimination taking place against an individual or group. Was this her greatest gift? Possibly. Although, now in our sixties (and occasionally stuck for something to do), Pam and I will still turn to one another and ask with wide-eyed bemusement: "Do you think Donald is out of jail yet?"

STEPHEN M. SILVERMAN (61)
New York, New York

Journaling Expedition #3

Forgiveness Letters

Married authors/counselors Joyce Vissel, RN, and Barry Vissel, MD, are staunch advocates of writing letters seeking forgiveness to loved ones you believe you have wronged. They describe the forgiveness letter as "one of the most powerful healing techniques we've ever come across." For the writer, it represents "an inner process of resolve and completion through taking responsibility and becoming vulnerable"—even if the letter is never sent (and it shouldn't always be). And for a potential recipient, say the Vissels, a letter of forgiveness can be better than a phone call or a face-to-face meeting, because it is "the least invasive or confrontive method. It doesn't put pressure on the recipient to respond or react in the moment. It allows time for reflection."

Here are the Vissels' guidelines for **crafting your own letter of forgiveness.** You can take notes in the various sections and use them as a jumping-off point for a letter to your adult child. © Copyright, July 2000 Shared Heart Foundation*(with permission) http://sharedheart.org/pages/powerfulforgiveness.htm*

1. Take responsibility for your part, how you hurt the other person, rather than give any attention to how they hurt you. In fact, if you haven't expressed your own hurt, this may need to be the first letter. However, for healing to be complete, you eventually need to take full responsibility for your own actions or even thoughts.

_____

_____

_____

_____

2. Be vulnerable. Reveal your own sadness or remorse for causing them pain.

_____

_____

_____

_____

3. Let them know you are not asking them to respond in any way. You are doing this for yourself, not to get forgiven by them. If they write back, it needs to clearly be their own choice.

_____

_____

_____

_____

4. If you can, include some appreciation for this person. Look at who they are rather than the painful interaction with you.

_____

_____

_____

_____

According to the Vissels, those are the four components of a forgiveness letter. You can also write your letter with the choice of not sending it. Asking for forgiveness is, after all, a very personal and internal process.

Now you can examine the following issues for yourself. *What are the pros and cons of sending the letter?*

_____

_____

_____

_____

Share the letter with someone you trust and get their feedback. *What was the feedback on it?*

_____

_____

_____

_____

If it feels right, send the letter. *What was your decision—to send or not to send? And how did it go?*

_____

_____

_____

_____

Are *you* ready to forgive an adult child's act that hurt you? Write an "I Forgive" letter. Some tips:

- Acknowledge your role in the issue.
- Be frank about the issue, but don't belabor your victimhood.
- Be sincere, not sarcastic.
- Let your love shine through and end on a positive, hopeful note.

_____

_____

_____

_____

_____

_____

_____

_____

Dr. Pinderman of the Mayo Clinic writes that it is important that we learn to forgive *ourselves,* as well:

> *Holding on to resentment against yourself can be just as toxic as holding on to resentment against someone else. Recognize that poor behavior or mistakes don't make you*

worthless or bad. Accept the fact that you—like everyone else—aren't perfect. Accept yourself despite your faults. Admit your mistakes. Commit to treating others with compassion, empathy and respect . . . Forgiveness of yourself or someone else, though not easy, can transform your life. Instead of dwelling on the injustice and revenge, instead of being angry and bitter, you can move toward a life of peace, compassion, mercy, joy and kindness.

What do you think you're ready to forgive yourself for, as a parent?

_____

_____

_____

_____

_____

CHAPTER IV

TLC ("TENDER LOVING COMMUNICATION"): THE GRANDEST WAY TO AVOID AND RESOLVE CONFLICT

"To put the world right in order, we must first put the nation in order; to put the nation in order, we must first put the family in order; to put the family in order, we must first cultivate our personal life; we must first set our hearts right."
—Confucius

Grandparenting with Love and Anxiety

Barbara is counting the days until she and her husband, Dave, become first-time grandparents. A startlingly clear sonogram picture of their grandson in utero is the cover image on their daughter Carrie's Facebook wall. His name will be Tyler. "I know it's crazy," says Barbara, "but I love him already!"

No seasoned grandparent considers this "crazy" at all.

Inside a wicker bassinet in the guest room, Barbara has collected her dreams for Tyler's first years: a christening gown that was his mother's; a collection of board books and stuffed animals; tiny rubber water shoes to protect tiny feet from hot sand and jagged shells. "Dave and I always loved taking Carrie to Jones Beach when she was growing up," she says, her eyes filling with tears. "Now we can't wait to take her little boy."

Like many of her friends who live near their adult children, Barbara (not her real name) has offered to care for her grandson several days a week after her daughter returns to work part-time. She is facing this new role with a heart full of love, anticipation, and no small amount of anxiety. Barbara is a very competent woman, but she's scared—really scared—she'll mess up.

"My own parents were extremely critical and overbearing, and I HATE when I hear myself 'butting in' just like they did," she admits. "Dave's folks—they were more reserved. But frankly, I want more of a connection with Tyler than they ever had with any of their grandchildren."

On the positive side, says Barbara, their relationship with daughter Carrie is in a good place now, after some difficult years during Carrie's teens and early twenties. And they are cordial with their son-in-law and his kin. Still, Barbara frets, "My friends keep telling me there's only one sure way to stay welcome in your children's and grandchildren's lives: **'Keep your mouth shut and your wallet open.'** A lot of the experts seem to agree! But do you really need to wear a permanent muzzle to be a good grandparent? Because, frankly, I don't know if I can manage that!"

Children Hear Parents' Voices in a Special Way

"Mouth shut/wallet open"—quite a strong prescription for preventing intergenerational conflicts. To be fair, it does contain some basic truths about human relations. *Nobody* appreciates tactless, relentlessly opinionated purveyors of unsolicited advice. And *everybody* appreciates people who are, to the best of their abilities, genuinely and joyfully generous, both materially and spiritually. In that sense, we should all go through life guarding our tongues and opening our "wallets" and hearts to support one another!

For many grandparents, however, the poignant observations of author Anne Roiphe will hit home. "Ah, my poor tongue is sore from being bitten," writes Roiphe in a grandparenting.com blog post, excerpted from an anthology of essays titled *Eye of My Heart (ed. Barbara Graham, Harper, 2010)*. Her well-intentioned advice is *never* welcomed, she points out ruefully:

When my daughter's first baby had colic and woke every 20 minutes, I suggested that she be left to cry a little while before being picked up. My daughter glared at me, a thousand daggers. "You would suggest that," she said, and burst into tears herself. I could see that my daughter was at her wits' end and could tolerate no suggestions at this tender, early stage of motherhood. She needed me to say, "You're doing everything right," which she was, essentially—or would be soon enough. I regretted my remark for the entire hour-long subway ride from her home back to my apartment.

I don't want to risk hurting my children, who hear my voice in a special way. A friend or neighbor can say almost anything without raising hackles. I can say almost nothing without causing pain. When I say, "I think the bath is too hot," I simply mean that the water may be too warm for the baby. But my daughters might hear me say, "You can't get the bath temperature right, what's the matter with you?" From me, my daughters want support, admiration, encouragement—and that is all they want. They have books, the internet and friends for everything else. (http://www.grandparents.com/family-and-relationships/inspiring-stories-and-wisdoms/contemporary-grandparenting-grandmotherhood)

Each one of us, at some time, has felt the pain of having a "sore tongue" like Anne Roiphe's. Nonetheless, I'm convinced that **we're headed in the wrong direction**—as families and as a society—if we embrace the notion that grandparents must serve as unequivocal cheerleaders who risk banishment if they express what's on their minds.

In the previous chapter, I observed that we grandparents are usually the ones who'll need to take the first step (and go the extra mile) on the path toward trust building and forgiveness in our families, being cautious of possible minefields in our relationships—areas where we may need to tread with more than the usual care. I'd say this comes with the territory of being human!

We've come a long way, thankfully, since the repressive and regressive decree that America's children should be "seen and not heard." Yet grandparents, not so long ago considered the wise old oracles, are now expected to remain silent.

Like most unbalanced relationship paradigms, it's ultimately a loss for all parties. But how do we achieve that elusive balance between overstepping our bounds and feeling muzzled? How do we steer clear of repeated, corrosive conflict, but still hear what's in each other's hearts?

Teaching-and-Learning Families Use "TLC"

Here's where my strong faith in the Teaching-and-Learning dynamic comes in. We are doing ourselves, our children, our grandchildren, and even future generations a disservice, if we're not actively teaching that there are other ways for families to communicate *besides* those problematic, polar opposites of yesteryear's unrestrained "Say Everything" and today's mandated "Say Nothing." I'm going to call it **speaking across the generations using "TLC"**—tender, loving communication.

The unfortunate paradox I've observed, through decades of observing families in crisis, is that a **reluctance** to speak candidly (but carefully) about areas of potential conflict **is the very thing** that *ensures* that eruptions of anger and hurt *will* occur, and makes the resultant discord that much harder to resolve. **Learning to discuss the tough stuff** *when times are good* **is what helps families build a foundation of trust, intimacy, and mutual understanding that can withstand life's storms.**

In Barbara's case, I suggested that she sit down with her husband, daughter, and son-in-law—perhaps in the context of calling for their very first Family Meeting—and use TLC to talk about what's on her mind *before* Tyler is born. After all, her self-confessed tendency to intrude with no-holds-barred commentaries isn't exactly a secret to the rest of her family; it was, in fact, a catalyst for a good deal of the enmity between her and her daughter in years gone by! Now it can become the catalyst for a frank conversation that creates positive ripples into the future.

Sharing her hopes and fears about this momentous life juncture not only helps Barbara to do and feel better. It also opens the door for each family member to examine and reveal their own concerns. In this mutually supportive atmosphere, they can start to discuss—even write down—some ground rules. They can be honest about each other's "non-negotiables." Carrie, for example, wants Barbara and Dave to purchase a car seat for their own vehicle and leave it installed at all times, so that there won't be last-minute scrambling when they want to take Tyler with them. And Barbara volunteers at a local hospice every Wednesday and has developed a special camaraderie with the personnel during her weekly shift; she'd like Carrie to take this into consideration and exempt her from having to babysit on Wednesdays.

TLC Respects Boundaries

Fruitful discussions enabled by Tender Loving Communication are far better predictors of intergenerational harmony and thriving connection than grim mandates like "mouth shut/wallet open." How much more there is for you, your children, and your grandchildren to look forward to, when you have "clear expectations/open hearts"—and a conscious commitment to keep TRYING, and keep talking, as your lives and circumstances change through the years.

Of course, for most of us, there's an unmistakable learning curve before we master TLC. It's an ongoing process that requires significantly more discipline and forethought than "Say Everything" if *that's* been your default mode through life! And it requires greater discernment and courage than simply resigning yourself to "Say Nothing."

TLC means asking ourselves some honest questions, and giving ourselves some honest answers, as we approach important conversations with our adult children and (as we and they grow) with our grandchildren. And the truth is: they're all important conversations!

Many new grandparents, like Barbara, feel immense uncertainty about what constitutes appropriate boundaries in their relationships with "the gatekeepers," a.k.a. their adult children. The number-one concern I hear voiced by today's grandparents is: **How do I know when it's appropriate to speak up about my concerns or opinions to my adult children, and when it isn't?**

The TLC Top Ten List

These common-sense questions can help you decide whether it's advisable to bring up a topic—using TLC, of course—or whether you're better off biting your tongue after all.

#1: *Am I TEACHING something of value, by saying it, or is it better left unsaid?*

For starters, I suggest that it may help to look to the words of twentieth century theologian Reinhold Niehbuhr (which were slightly adapted to become the iconic "Serenity Prayer" used by Twelve-Step programs). One does not need to be a person of faith to embrace its wisdom:

> **God give me grace to accept with Serenity the things that cannot be changed;**
> **Courage to change the things which should be changed;**
> **And Wisdom to distinguish the one from the other.**

Be honest with yourself in asking: **What is my purpose in making this statement to my child?** Are you speaking up in order to promote a family-member's welfare—and it's perfectly legitimate if it's your *own* welfare!—or to correct a genuine misunderstanding, or right a true wrong? Or are you following an impulse to be controlling? Furthering an agenda of your personal prejudices or unreasonable expectations?

Being un-muzzled does not give a parent or grandparent license to "bite." For example, if your loved one has experienced a crushing disappointment, telling him or her "I told you so" (or its equivalent) does nobody any good.

#2: WHEN should I say it?

In general, it is better *not* to delve into hot-button issues during times of high emotion; wait until things have calmed down. In years past, when my children were raising their children, they would sometimes phone me to offload a litany of parenting concerns. Very rarely did they ask for my opinion; they simply wanted to let off steam. I often felt I had useful advice for them—some insights that might help—based on my professional knowledge and my years of parenting *them*! But all those years of experience had taught me something else too: highly agitated individuals are seldom receptive to unasked-for prescriptions for how to fix things. They're much more likely to shoot the messenger.

#3: So how will I know if it's the RIGHT time to say it?

Herein lies the essence of our Teaching-and-Learning paradigm: you'll know, because you ASK. To this day, if my children or older grandchildren share a vexing problem with me, I say, very calmly, the following:

> "Would you like me to tell you what I think? Or should I choose a better time? Or should I say nothing at all?"

And then I abide by their answer, without challenging it. If it's clear that the problem is persisting, I'll bring it up at a time that is less emotionally charged and ask again if they want to hear my ideas. It's important that they know I respect them as competent, independent adults. This is key to all of us being able to embrace our alternating roles as teachers and learners.

#4: HOW *do I say it?*

Above all: tactfully. In chapter 2, we spoke of the importance of interacting with gentleness and kindness during Family Meetings. This isn't a tall order if we *always* make a conscious effort to address each other that way. It never ceases to amaze me that we seem to speak more graciously and respectfully with complete strangers than we do with our own families! Charitable, compassionate speech begins at home. Caustic language, sarcastic subtexts, accusatory assumptions—these have no place in our discourse. **If the walls of your home really did "have ears" and could talk, what would they say about the way you speak to each other?**

#5: *Should I say it in PRIVATE?*

Family Meetings can be a good forum to bring up topics that are difficult to discuss; some family members can inspire others with the courage to speak frankly. But in certain instances, privacy may be more appropriate. When in doubt: here, too, ASK. The more comfortable you become with "asking" instead of "assuming," the fewer faux pas you will make.

#6: *Must I say it in PERSON?*

There's a school of thought that important issues should always be raised face-to-face, and certainly there are situations in which it would be cowardly or insensitive to do otherwise. And often, a sympathetic look, big hug, or gentle smile will greatly reduce a listener's antagonism.

Interestingly, studies have shown that your adult child's gender can play a role in how receptive he or she may be to various modes of in-person interaction. Studies have shown that women tend to prefer face-to-face conversations, with a preference to sitting across a corner of a table; direct "confrontational" talking triggers primate fight/flight responses. Males tend to prefer side-by-side conversation, like sitting together in the front seat of a car.

#7: Is it ever BETTER to say it over the phone or email?

I have observed that family members sometimes find it easier to delve into uncomfortable topics via telephone. And there are times that expressing ideas in a carefully crafted letter or email will enable you to present them without interruption and give your child or grandchild time to process before responding. That said, putting delicate matters in writing can come back to haunt you; plus, they can also be forwarded to parties with whom you had no intention of sharing your personal business. Weigh your words very, very carefully before you hit the "send" button.

#8: If I inadvertently cause PAIN by what I do or say, how do I take responsibility and learn from it?

It's inevitable: we who TRY will occasionally fail. Even the most loving families fall prey to missteps and misunderstandings. The trick is in how these painful events are handled. A family whose members actively endorse a **culture of forgiveness** will make mutual understanding its highest priority; they will not tolerate grudges, excessive blaming or shaming, or protracted periods of estrangement. (Although taking a little breather after a serious disagreement can help all parties to cool down and gain perspective.) If your actions cause ill will, regardless of how well-intended they were, apologize immediately and make sure you ask what was hurtful about your actions so that you understand (without making assumptions) why this occurred.

Perhaps there is a pattern in your behavior or speech that you need to address; as a Learner, you need to be open to this. It's possible too that you struck a nerve that has nothing to do with you; and in responding to your questions about what went wrong, your adult child or grandchild may recognize some issues they would do well to address. Each of us owns our own individual, intensely personal, and idiosyncratic history of our family. If we don't make an effort to share those histories, we will forever remain mysteries to each other.

#9: If I'M the one stung or confused by my children's or grandchildren's words or actions, am I able to Teach by candidly sharing what I'm feeling?

Grandma and Grandpa can have hurt feelings too. One would hope that at our stage in life, we are above pettiness in our interpersonal relations. At the same time, we are not robots or doormats. I confess to having felt slighted recently when I tried reaching one of my grandchildren several times over the course of a week, and he did not return any of my calls. When he finally did call, he explained apologetically that he had been very busy, traveling and coordinating an academic conference. Now it was my opportunity to Teach about forgiveness. I candidly shared my hurt feelings, while at the same time reflecting on the fact that I should have been more patient and understanding, and not have taken his slow response so personally. **Honest conversations about adverse emotions or interactions can also create opportunities for enhanced closeness; they need not be swept under the rug.**

#10: But how do we fully resolve conflict if it DOES arise?

Conflict is an inevitable part of being a family—of being human. Episodic conflict will not destroy a strong family. This brings us (again) full circle to the family's culture of forgiveness. But there's more to it than that. Harmonious families triumph over conflict by giving it a double whammy. Its members are both **"slow to anger *and* quick to forgive."** These attributes, which are cornerstones of all the world's religions, are among the most valuable ones for us, as family elders, to role-model in our own behavior and interactions.

Don't we all know people who go through life being *quick* to anger and *slow* to forgive? These unhappy souls are primed to swoop down upon and magnify every perceived slight and believe the worst of everyone. Instead of striving to be consensus-builders and peace-seekers, they appear driven to divide, conquer, and control. They corner you with tedious, bitter rants about being perpetually wronged, victimized by ungrateful family members, mean-spirited employers, incompetent service people.

Older adults who fixate on how others treat them, with little concern about how they treat others, will inevitably isolate themselves. On the other hand, it's hard for even the most curmudgeonly family member to stay mad at a grandparent with a generally upbeat disposition, a generous heart, and a ready sense of humor.

If you and your family can resist pouring your collective energies into the black hole of acrimony and recrimination, you've won half the battle toward achieving The Grandest Love.

Recently, at the funeral of the wife of a dear friend, the adult children and teenage grandson told wonderful stories about how important she was in their lives. They spoke about the values she imparted, the love she gave them through good times and bad. As they spoke, I wondered whether they had ever said these things to her while she was alive—while they were growing up, or as adults.

I think that part of Tender Loving Communication is for us grandparents to teach our family members, the importance of saying the things that should be said while we're still around. We need to tell each other what we mean to each other—not save it for eulogies after we're gone. The obligation isn't towards those who attend our funerals. We should express our love to each other, unselfconsciously and gratefully, while we're alive.

THE GRANDCHILDREN SPEAK

NEVER A WORD IN ANGER

My work for a judge required me to read probation reports that detail a convict's life. They seem to teach that evil produces evil. Burglars often knew poverty as children. Drug users had the poison forced on them. Murderers, invariably, were abused as children.

So how is it, then, that my maternal grandmother, Rita Friedman (1928-2010), so thoroughly defied this apparent law of human nature to emerge a spirit of grace, humility, sweetness, and elegance? She was raised in Stalin's Russia. She endured a cruel stepfather. Her studies were interrupted by Hitler's invasion of the Ukraine; she was evacuated east, but much of her family was executed by Nazis behind a tractor factory in Kharkov. All before she was twenty years old.

Yet none of us ever heard her speak a word in anger or resentment. Her delight was to encourage us in honorable pursuits; our delight was to present her with the fruits of that encouragement. I was eight when she first gave me a pen to chronicle our long, happy summers together in Vineland, New Jersey. From that day on, through my schooling and work as a journalist, until the hour of her death, I sent her not only every item I wrote, but every note I received in response.

She was an angel to us in life, and is one now. Her memory reminds me every day that happiness is not the consequence of facts around us, but a state of soul within—and it is a choice.

JOSEPH FRIEDMAN TARTAKOVSKY (31)
San Francisco, California

YOU MAKE ME SMILE!

Papa Harvey, you've taught me to see humor in every situation. You take any problem or argument and find a way to make the other person laugh. Grandma sometimes gets frustrated by this, but I think it lightens the mood, and it puts a smile on my face!

KAYLEE
Pelham Jewish Community HS

"YIZKOR" (MEMORIAL) SERMON

This time of year, the High Holy Days, I am filled with nostalgia. As Rabbi Shira Milgrom writes: *"Yom Kippur brings us back to memory. We let ourselves sit amidst the powerful memories of those with whom we have lived our lives—those who gave us life, or perhaps those with whose legacy we still wrestle, or those whose love continues to nurture us."*

The memories we so often turn back to this time of year are memories of time spent with family. This past June I visited the city, which I was born: Chicago, Illinois. I not only love going back there because it is where I spent the first nine years of my life, but also because it is where my mom's side of the family is from. And while most of them—my grandparents, my Uncle Russell, and others—are no longer living, I feel their presence when I am in that city and a strong connection to their memory.

I sometimes feel mad that I didn't have enough time with these relatives, mad that some died at such a young age and mad that I was too young to understand how to value the time with them while they were alive. And at the same time I am grateful. I am grateful that they existed. That they impacted my life in various ways and that their memory is for a blessing.

But I still find myself thinking, "What I wouldn't do to have one more conversation . . ." to ask all the questions I now have, at 33; to get to show them who I am. For them to see the woman I became from the girl they knew.

Sometimes I feel them with me. My grandfather, Carl Lerner, aka "Pop," had a wooden statue of a guy standing on a log, fishing. That statue is now in my apartment. And sometimes when I look up at that man fishing, I sense my grandfather in the room. I believe it is his spirit, or some manifestation of his spirit, that is in that wood. Maybe because it lived in his bedroom for so long his energy is still on it. Or maybe it's my own projection of his memory onto it. Whatever it is, I am happy that the possibility exists to feel his presence—and I am glad that I am open to that experience.

*   *   *

The Yizkor service is a time of remembering and honoring the dead and also a time for us to bring to mind or to recreate, if only for a few brief moments, the connections that once existed. Sometimes experiencing these connections feels as if our loved ones are still with us . . . and how comforting this is.

Memory is a gift, something we must not take for granted. In Rabbi Milgrom's words: *"Sometimes, the eye of memory sees things more clearly than can be seen in life itself."* And Leila Gal Berner says: *"Whenever we take time to think about our origins, or go back to the home where we spent our childhood, we find that things have changed. The years have taken their toll. Death has taken away many of the people who filled our early years. And yet—if only in our deepest memories, home continues to be with us. We carry our ancestors and our homes through all the years of our lives. We cannot go home again, but if we can remember, we are never really away from home."*

Yom Kippur—and this particular moment, the Yizkor of Yom Kippur—is a time to remember. Perhaps, if we cannot feel the presence of our loved ones physically with us, we can do our best to go back to our time with them. Because even if bodies don't endure, love does. And maybe that is what Pop's wooden statue of a man fishing is all about. It is a manifestation of love.

I will never forget the one and only time I went fishing. It was with Pop. I was the only girl on the boat with a bunch of older fellows in Florida, and I caught the biggest fish. So big that the boat staff had to come help me reel it in. And I think my grandfather was quite impressed and proud.

That memory stays with me. That memory is love.

RABBI MOLLY G. KANE
Brooklyn, New York

Journaling Expedition #4:

Developing a "TLC" Dialogue

This exercise challenges you to examine some of the issues you've considered raising with your adult offspring and to practice sharing them using Tender Loving Communication. Note: the exercise can be adapted for dialogues between grandparents and (older) grandchildren; between in-laws, spouses, siblings, etcetera.

To get you started, here are three sample issues, presented in:

- A **"Bite-Your-Tongue" version,** which demonstrates how we sound when we speak carelessly, without TLC, i.e., making statements that could easily wound feelings and spark conflict.

- A **"TLC" version** that conveys the emotional truth of what's on our minds and speaks to others' hearts.

And finally:

- **A potential "TLC Response"** — an illustration of the type of dialogue we open the door to when we address our loved ones with TLC.

At the bottom, there is space for you to insert some questions you've crafted and for your family member to respond, if desired, to the issues you raised.

SAMPLE QUESTION #1:

> **BITE YOUR TONGUE:** "Do you know how *long* it's been since you made the time to go anywhere with me, without an entourage? I don't mind going to the kids' activities sometimes, but does everything always have to revolve around them and their activities? You never do anything besides work and go to their games!"

- *TLC:* "Son, every once in a while, when it's convenient for you, I'd love the opportunity for some alone-time with you—a dinner out, a walk; a time when we can talk about adult topics—the family, politics, etc. I'd love to know your thoughts about the stock market, and what you've been reading lately."

- *Possible response:* "I'd really like that too, Dad. Let me check with Cheryl first, and then we can set up a regular get-together, maybe Sunday brunch, once a month. How about that new diner near your apartment?"

SAMPLE QUESTION #2:

> *BITE YOUR TONGUE:* "Don't think I didn't see you and Cheryl rolling your eyes last week when that TV show came on about teen drug use, and I started talking about it with Jayden! You treat him like a baby! Well, guess what: kids that age aren't babies anymore! Why do I have to pussyfoot around everything? Every time I open my mouth, you guys make a face!"

- *TLC:* "Now that Jayden's almost in middle school, I wonder whether you have strong feelings about what role you hope I will play in his life. Like, are there things I did or said while you were growing up that you are eager for me to share or do with him? Or the opposite: are there ways I interacted with to you that you prefer I do not repeat?"

- *Possible response:* "Glad you brought that up, Dad. In fact, Jayden's been having some difficulties lately with the concept of God, and I think that being able to open up to you about religion would be helpful to him. Also, I'm going to ask you, please, not to mention that DUI arrest I had during college. I haven't figured out when or how—or if—to tell him, and maybe you and I can discuss that. But I do know I want the story to come from me, not from you."

SAMPLE QUESTION #3:

> *BITE YOUR TONGUE:* "Your mother's been gone almost five years now, may she rest in peace—and I must've asked FIFTY times for somebody to come and help me clean out that attic space where she kept her sewing materials. I know everybody's busy, but I have to start thinking of myself, maybe selling the house; what the heck's gonna become of ME, if I can't get anybody to give me a few lousy hours to deal with her stuff?"

- *TLC:* **"Kids, I want us to feel comfortable discussing what may lie ahead for me as I grow old. I'd like to be able to talk to you about my concerns about aging, disability, quality-of-life and end-of-life issues; and I want to hear *your* thoughts too. I don't plan on going anywhere soon, but it would be a big load off my mind to start putting some thoughts on paper about all this, and wrapping up some loose ends in the house."**

- *Possible response:* "This is a tough one for me, Dad. It would be easier for me if Cheryl could be in on these conversations too, at least to get the ball rolling. I know you value her input too, so I really hope that works for you! And look, I'm sorry I never got to the attic cleanup you asked me to do. It wasn't only that I didn't have time—I just couldn't deal with it. I think Cheryl will take Mom's sewing machine now; the kids are a little older, and I think they'll enjoy making Halloween costumes with her, just like I used to with Mom."

*   *   *

Your TLC Teaching-and-Learning Dialogue

Here are some things I'd really like you to know, Son/Daughter, along with how much I love you; and I'd like to hear what you think too.

QUESTION #1:

_____
_____
_____
_____

*Response:*_____
_____
_____
_____
_____
_____
_____

QUESTION #2:

_____
_____
_____
_____

*Response:*_____
_____
_____
_____
_____
_____
_____

QUESTION #3:

_____

_____

_____

_____

*Response:*_____

_____

_____

_____

_____

_____

_____

_____

CHAPTER V

THE GRAND BALANCE:
DECLARING OUR INTERDEPENDENCE

"If the family were a fruit, it would be an orange, a circle of sections, held together but separable—each segment distinct."
—Letty Cottin Pogrebin

"Diversity: the art of thinking independently, together."
—Malcolm Forbes

Independence: It's the American Way

In 2010, I took an adult-education course at Northwestern University, titled "Families in the 21st Century." My fellow students were, for the most part, the baby-boomer parents of young-adult offspring. And I observed a very interesting phenomenon. During our classroom discussions, nobody had a problem intellectually embracing "collectivism" as a powerful, twenty-first-century *political* value; we all agreed that nations could benefit immensely from sharing resources and developing joint initiatives in such critical areas as global economic development and climate research.

But when it came to *personal* values and family living, an altogether different paradigm prevailed. **Independence and auto-**

nomy were prized above all else, and the flip side—immediately labeled as "dependence"—elicited shudders all around. As it happened, a number of these parents were experiencing the phenomenon of "boomerang kids." They were distraught that their empty nests had recently been refilled by twenty-somethings who were unemployed or underemployed and behaving like spoiled teens—borrowing the car without refilling the gas tank, having friends over who pillaged the refrigerator and liquor cabinet, leaving around their messes and dirty laundry.

I validated my classmates' frustration but pointed out what I thought was obvious: that setting basic ground rules and coming up with some creative alternatives could transform shared living during economically challenging times, into a win-win situation. Grown children could contribute by setting up technology networks, cleaning out the garage, and shredding old documents, for example. Household chores should be divided so that the burdens would be less on everyone, and developing imaginative menus might become an enjoyable shared activity. I wasn't blind to the challenges of having kids boomerang back home, but truthfully, it didn't sound so terrible to be able to go for an occasional after-dinner walk with an offspring I'd never expected to have under my roof again.

And wasn't it possible that the regressive, inappropriate behavior my classmates were observing, may have been rooted in their kids' anxiety about the economic hand that America's millenials have been dealt? Maybe it could help everybody in the family to talk more about their own fears, embarrassment, and expectations?

"Well, I want them out of the house!" one father responded firmly to my comments. *"Independent is the thing to be."* Most of the others nodded vociferously in agreement. Even the professor didn't dispute the notion that lacking a firm grip on the brass ring of independence—a proud, all-American virtue if ever there was one!—clearly represented some sort of failure, weakness, or sin.

I realized then that in our "pull-yourself-up-by-your-bootstraps" culture, we have become so deeply wary of being, becoming or even appearing *dependent*, that we often overlook—and stigmatize—one of our most gloriously human and important Family Values: **interdependence.**

Interdependence Helps Families Stay Strong

There's no question that human beings possess an innate pull towards independent action, individuality, and self-determination, and that it is critical that each of us acquire the skills and the confidence to live successfully on our own and transmit those values to the next generations. I don't think that there's a single reader of this book who I have to sell on the importance of cultivating one's personal independence! Let's take that as a given, shall we? **But the ability to depend on others when necessary—especially our families—for physical, emotional, and economic support is no less important to our survival than being able to go it alone, nor is it less noble.** We need the skills, the courage, and the good sense to know how to do both at the appropriate junctures.

Stephen Covey expressed it perfectly in *The 7 Habits of Highly Effective People*:

> *Independent thinking alone is not suited to interdependent reality. Independent people who do not have the maturity to think and act interdependently may be good individual producers, but they won't be good leaders or team players. They're not coming from the paradigm of interdependence necessary to succeed in marriage, family, or organizational reality.*

Years of personal and professional experience have convinced me that **families who recognize their interdependence are more likely to be responsive, resilient, and able to manage the unexpected.** Comfortably embracing interdependence frees us to create a family life characterized by connectedness, trust, kindness, mutual respect, and the ability to traverse various roles, without fanfare, as circumstances change and needs arise. When we've eliminated blaming and shaming, there is no need to judge each other or ourselves when the need for support arises as it will, at some time or another, for nearly all of us.

Just as we value serving alternately as Teachers and Learners within our families, we need, too, to practice moving back and forth fluidly between being Givers and Takers—each in his or her time, each according to his or her ability. And if we embrace this fluidity of roles as a matter of course, it won't be such an awful shock to the family system if and when it becomes necessary to give or take *more*—like when someone suddenly loses a job. Or a house. Or their once-robust health.

Paradoxically, becoming at ease with mutual interdependence can actually help family members build up their individual strengths, competencies, and self-reliance. When others have stepped up to the plate for you, you want (if humanly possible) to become a person who is able and willing to step up to the plate for others.

A Cultural Basis for Interdependence

In many cultures, of course, interdependence is woven into the fabric of family life and doesn't need to be promoted as a positive value. This is apparent among immigrant families—for practical reasons as well as historical ones—as well as others in our midst who cling to highly traditional cultural, ethnic, or religious values. "Boomeranging" is the norm, and extended families frequently live under one roof to reduce expenses.

Maybe such practices harken back to your own beloved Yéye, Ojiisan, Babcia, or Abuelo. Then you know too that as such families assimilated, their standards and expectations became more aligned with an exalted American dream that prizes individual attainments and comfort above communal obligation.

There appear to be, however, some marked socioeconomic trends indicating that interdependence is making a comeback—and not just among immigrant families. In a still-faltering economy, with altered definitions of what families look like, grandparents are playing a stronger role than ever in the lives of their children and grandchildren.

Times (and Families) Are Changing

Some eye-opening statistics from the 2011 MetLife Report on American Grandparents:

- Just over one in ten grandparents (13%) provides care on a regular basis for at least one grandchild. Of those, 32% are babysitting/caregiving five or more days per week; 15% are raising at least one grandchild.

- Among children younger than five whose mothers worked outside the home, 30% are cared for on a regular basis by a grandparent during their mother's working hours (2005 figures). (*http://www.census.gov/newsroom/releases/archives/children/cb08-31.html*)

- The majority (62%) of grandparents have provided financial support or monetary gifts for grandchildren within the past five years. Of those grandparents who provide financial assistance:

  - The average amount given for all grandchildren over the past five years was $8,289 total. More than half gave up to $5,000.

  - Cash was the most common type of financial support, and helping with basic needs rose to the top with 43% of grandparents giving for clothing, 33% for general support, and 29% for education, such as preschool through private high school, tutoring, college tuition, and graduate school.

- Forty-three percent report they are providing more financial support because of the economic downturn, and one-third (34%) are giving financial support to grandchildren, even though they believe it is having a negative effect on their own financial security.

Even multigenerational living is making a comeback. According to a report by the Pew Research Center:

> *As of 2008, a record 49 million Americans, or 16.1% of the total U.S. population, lived in a family household that contained at least two adult generations or a grandparent and at least one other generation . . . This represents a significant trend reversal. Starting right after World War II, the extended family household fell out of favor with the American public. In 1940, about a quarter of the population lived in one; by 1980, just 12% did.*
> *(http://www.pewsocialtrends.org/2010/03/18/the-return-of-the- multi-generational-family-household/)*

Pooling resources by moving in together after unemployment, lost stock-market gains, dwindling pensions, and housing foreclosures has its win-win aspects. The biggest winners are the grandchildren, according to Amy Goyer, senior vice president for outreach for Grandparents.com, writing for AARP. org:

> *Children get some extra-special attention from loving adults . . . people who [grow] up with grandparents living in their homes seem to know them on a more personal level . . . [G]randparents tend to be central characters in these grandkids' life stories, as opposed to part of the peripheral supporting cast. A sense of generational responsibility and the importance of transferring knowledge across the generations are well ingrained. Family history and cultural heritage are constant companions to members of multigenerational households.*
> *(http://womensissues.about.com/od/startingover/a/ MomMovesStats.htm)*

What's so Scary about Interdependence?

Let's face it: life cycle changes are humbling. Even happy changes, like becoming a grandparent, force us to face certain realties that we may not be ready for. After all these years at the helm, we've gotten very accustomed to our leadership role as The Parents. Oh, sure, we've been practicing the fine art of "letting go" from the first time we put our kids on a school bus! Still, it's tough. **Because NOTHING can change the fact that for as long as we live, we will always be their parents, and they will always be our children.**

Even with all the years of changes and adjustments in our parent-child relationships, the arrival of a grandchild signals an entirely new era. The circle of life has turned, and now there are two sets of parents in the room: them and us. The profound delight we evince as we gaze upon this new being also carries with it some fear and loss we're not used to thinking about or expressing. Suddenly, we feel old, no longer in charge; and there are so many unknowns. *How welcomed will I be into the life of this new family? Have I done a good job in transmitting my most deeply felt values; do I even have a right to care whether they'll be upheld, or is that too controlling? If I help them too much, am I infantilizing them, "enabling?"* And *what will happen to me as I age? Will I be able to take care of myself? If I ask for help, am I weak?*

We're not the only ones feeling like we've aged overnight. Look deep into your children's eyes; sure, they're over-the-moon, sleep-deprived, and scared. *Do I have the maturity to be a parent, a partner, a provider? If I ask my parents for help, does it mean that I'm dependent again, and they can treat me like a child, exert dominance over me? I mean, I'll always be their kid! But what if they get sick? Can I care for them* and *for my growing family?*

What often happens then, in too many families, is that **the fear wins.** Parents and adult children institute a knee-jerk, misguided "Declaration of Independence" because they believe that's what's supposed to happen now. Don't share what's troubling you. Don't ask for what you need. *Don't tell Mom!* This leads to mutual frustration and guardedness, futile attempts at mind-reading, personal implosions and interpersonal explosions—events that breed miscommunication and distance at precisely the times that frankness and durable connections are needed most.

I think it's more true than ever, these days: families must make an active commitment to discuss important issues openly and respectfully, or they may find themselves in a most unpleasant predicament: struggling fiercely to maintain some semblance of independence, or succumbing to "interdependence" that is filled with nonstop conflict—i.e., a situation that could really spiral into the kind of unbalanced *dependence* that most families want to avoid.

The first thing to do (if you fear you may be headed in that direction) is to take a deep breath. *Acknowledging our changed reality—that we've all entered a new stage of life—and talking about it is a first step to defusing the fears that accompany it.* This does not happen all at once; it happens in, well, baby steps. Patience, compassion, humor, and the belief that we are not diminished by interdependent relationships, will keep us strong and secure as individuals and as a nurturing family unit.

My own family's interdependence was certainly put to the test on a number of occasions. There were periods during which family members became unemployed, and Margaret and I helped financially—paying several mortgage payments, buying a used car, making sure the grandkids could stay in school or have childcare. When Margaret became ill, we were the ones who had to ask for help. I spent eight years as a caregiver, and there were situations in which I felt I needed additional support from my children and grandchildren. Those twice-a-year Family Meetings became our forums for discussing the "new normal" that now prevailed in our lives, sparking conversations that would continue and evolve in the intervening months. **We all had to learn to ask for what we needed.**

Don't Let Your Resources Get Too Thin

Part of healthy interdependence is also for family members to understand that they have a right—even an obligation—to say "no" to requests for help that they cannot handle, and to do so lovingly before burnout occurs or resentments fester. This is a delicate balance that—unless there is clear, open communication—can teeter over to unhealthy enabling, or to excessive dependence. Generally speaking, adult children need to place the needs of their partners, their young families, and their employment *first*. And grandparents should not compromise their own financial security, physical or emotional health, or marital harmony by overextending themselves for adult children or grandchildren. As sincerely as grandparents may wish to help out, and as much as they may cherish one-on-one time with the little ones, not every older adult is cut out to babysit (especially for very young children) for protracted periods. Sometimes well-meaning grandparents agree to provide childcare on a regular basis without realizing, at first, that they've bitten off more than they can chew. Other times, harried adult children keep expanding the scope of work beyond what was agreed upon. Unfortunately, one all too often hears exhausted grandparents complaining to their friends and associates about feeling taken advantage of, instead of them sitting down with their children to try and come up with workable alternatives.

As you've surely gathered by now, **I'm the world's biggest cheerleader for making conscious grandparenting a key priority in your life—but this does not mean making grandparenting *your life*.** That would be unwise, unfair, and unhealthy for you and for the rest of your family. Part of your role in a Teaching-and-Learning family is to role-model how to remain a vibrant and contributing member of your community, as much as your health and circumstances will allow. Whether you are still working or retired: exercise regularly, eat well, stay on top of your finances, take a class, start a book club, volunteer. If you are one of the thousands of American grandparents who have uprooted themselves (or plan to) in order to live closer to adult children or grandchildren, actively seek ways to become involved and make friends in your new surroundings, rather than relying solely on the kids for your social life. Recent studies indicate that strong interpersonal connections are a key factor in longevity and in healthier, more fulfilling aging. *(nytimes.com/2012/09/12/business/retirementspecial/for-older-adults-close-connections-are-key-to-healthy-aging.html?_r=0)*

Of course, should unexpected tragedy strike, even our most carefully tended plans are often dashed to pieces, or at least back-burnered. When we or our loved ones are in crisis, triage is typically the only workable approach.

How Can Grandparents Help?

Cultivating healthy interdependence is not about being demanding or seeking control. In good times, it's about seeking natural entry-points where we can connect with our children and grandchildren—**entry-points we discover by taking a genuine interest in their lives and activities.** It sounds absurdly simple, doesn't it? Yet it's surprising how few grandparents consciously, actively ask questions that are anything but perfunctory. Or their questions smack of built-in expectations and judgments. *Did you win? How many goals did you score?*

Cultivating and displaying genuine curiosity about who your grandchildren are as individuals, and what their world is like, and letting them Teach you, is among the best investments you can make in your family's future. **Be committed to spend some alone-time with each of them, even if it's just going for an ice-cream cone together.** Hear what matters to them and what they think is funny; watch TV with them and listen to their music. This will help you develop a shared vocabulary. And tell them your stories; you are the historian of their past. And they will bring those stories into the future, to generations you may not see.

America's changing family landscape means that many of us have—or will someday acquire—step-grandchildren. Make it a point to give them alone-time too. You may not initially feel the same connection to newly acquired step-grandchildren that you have with those you've known since they came into the world. That's okay; you don't have to advertise it. When you have a big heart, feelings grow to fill it. I know many grandparents who have developed wonderful relationships with step-grandkids through the years. But this requires making *more* of an effort to consistently connect with them, not less. **One of the very best ways you can support your adult child, and help to ensure the success of his or her new marriage, is to embrace every member of this blended family with interest and enthusiasm.**

Ties with Teens Strengthen Families and Communities

As my own grandchildren got older, it became clear that maintaining strong connections was increasingly challenging as their schedules grew more demanding and their academics, extracurriculars, and friendships predominated. Something else was clear too: **that the high school years are a critical period during which close bonds with caring family members are more important than ever.** At the same time that our grandchildren are demanding autonomy and privacy, they may be grappling with issues that can be intensely overwhelming: challenging new academic undertakings and social pressures, drivers licenses, and first-time employment; drug and alcohol use, sexual behavior and gender-identity questions, to name but a few. Knowing what is happening in their world, in their school, creates context for discussion; you can log onto their high school's website to keep abreast of what is going on in their community, and to be able to inquire about their sports teams or theatrical productions, regardless of how far away you live. **Sometimes a teenager will feel more comfortable confiding in an empathic, nonjudgmental grandparent than in a parent.** (Even after they go off to college, you can access their school's website and read their school paper online. For additional insights into the world of your college-age grandchildren, see http://collegetipsforparents.org/.)

Recognizing that these years are such critical ones for young people, I approached the administration of our local public school, Deerfield High, with an idea to create a "Grandparents' Orientation Day" as part of the annual back-to-school programming. I couldn't have hoped for a more enthusiastic buy-in from the school's administration. Beginning with the freshman year and continuing through all four years of a student's high-school career, grandparents will be invited to meet their grandchildren's teachers and to hear a panel of students (from the subsequent grade) discuss what the new academic year will entail. Each month, they are kept abreast of what's going on at Deerfield, including coursework, sports, theater, and other extracurricular activities, via a student-produced e-newsletter, "The Grand Connection," that is posted every month on the school's website, http://dhs.dist113.org/parents/Pages/Grandparents.aspx.

Thanks to the hugely positive response to this program, I've begun working with several other Chicago-area schools, both public and private, who have expressed interest in creating similar initiatives.

Whether or not it would benefit your own grandchildren, if volunteerism is in your blood, you might consider approaching a high school in your area to see if they would be interested in launching such a program. Becoming involved in your local school system or in an organization that promotes joint social-action activities with youth is an excellent investment in a stronger and more connected community. And nothing keeps you young like being around young people!

Interaction Enhances Interdependence!

Since none of my grandchildren live nearby and I only see them several times a year, I try and schedule a weekly phone call with each of them. This past year, Aidan, the youngest, shared his excitement over his upcoming tenth birthday. "Listen to this, Grandpa," he announced proudly, "I'm becoming a *two-digit boy!*" I found it quite touching that Aidan had managed to find something special about this birthday, because it was coming at a time of other events that might've eclipsed it; his older sister was soon to celebrate her Bat Mitzvah, and his oldest brother had recently been married. That week, when I spoke to the other grandchildren, I made a point of telling them that Aidan had given himself this new nickname. He was overjoyed when several of them contacted him with birthday wishes for "Two-Digit Boy." It was a small gesture, really. But it made him feel wonderful that the big kids had reached out to him. It made him feel *somebody's listening. What I say matters.*

A few years from now, Aidan may barely recall that he took such pleasure in turning two digits. A slew of greater preoccupations will assume center stage in his busy life. My hope is that he will keep sharing those ideas with the rest of us. Because we all remain "two-digit" people for a long, long time; and through that time we keep growing and changing, winning and losing, struggling and adapting. And it's easier when you know you are not alone, that regardless of your circumstances, or how far you may travel, you will always be part of an unbreakable chain of love.

THE GRANDCHILDREN SPEAK

FIRST MY HAND . . . THEN GRANDPA'S

When I was little, my paternal grandfather, Abe, and I enjoyed many hours of playing Rummy at his kitchen table. First, my grandfather would conduct the impressive table shuffle, then the mystifying riffle shuffle and then the cards would be flicked out—dealt one by one to each player. Next, "the gathering of the cards" . . . where you familiarize yourself with the cards you've been dealt with and strategize how you will proceed.

While the "big kids" quickly made their choices of which cards to keep, I would always need a bit more time. Grandpa would always wait so patiently for me to complete my turn—which is not an easy thing to do. Ever try playing Rummy with a six-year-old? Poor Gramps had to endure my eight-minute turns—four minutes to decide which card to get rid of and four minutes to arrange the cards in my hand so I could see what I had to work with.

Grandpa noticed my frustration stemming from not being able to hold all of the cards in my hand. With an eye for "fixing," he disappeared for a few minutes. After a few clanks and clangs from spelunking through his kitchen, he returned to the table with a million-dollar idea. He took two plastic coffee can lids, stapled them together in the middle and placed the cards in fan-like fashion, and voila! My very own personal card-holder!

I proudly held that cardholder filled with my cards spread out in a beautiful fan of black spades and red diamonds, of kings and queens and oh my . . . this was a whole new card game! I'll never forget the sense of pure fascination, watching in awe how my grandfather so quickly thought of a solution—creating something from nothing.

Thanks to Grandpa's ingenuity, the once anxiety-provoking situation of decision-making was now time spent bonding with a loved one, making the experience far more enjoyable to play (for everyone).

My grandparents, as Holocaust survivors, had become experts at relying on themselves because they were forced to. It was their quick, out-of-the box thinking that led them to survive the incredible hardships they experienced. We have much to learn from their incredible sense of self-reliance.

The seed was planted in my mind—to approach life with an intention to make the best of any situation by working smarter, not necessarily harder. These days, visits with my grandfather are still filled with the same amount of love and laughter as when I was a child, but where there once were many joys, there are a lot more "oys." I've watched how the cruel hands of time have left their marks on 93-year-old Grandpa. It's hard to watch him struggle to remember things, not being able to participate in conversations because of his hearing loss, and witnessing the constant "it's-on-the-tip-of-my-tongue" look on his face.

I am always trying to find activities that empower him and give him a sense of autonomy. And while there aren't many, I have learned that although his verbal abilities may not be what they once were—the man can still play a round of Rummy.

Recently, our family played 14-card Rummy together—and while we'd quickly make our decisions, when it got to my grandpa's turn, we'd wait . . . and wait and I noticed he was struggling to keep his cards together in his hand. They kept falling out when he tried to see what cards he was dealing with, leading to a sense of frustration that looked all too familiar.

Just then, a cartoon light-bulb appeared above my head. "I'll be right back," I said, and went scurrying through the kitchen drawers and found two lids from the "The Kosher Nosh Deli," stapled 'em in the middle and arranged his cards in a fan-like manner. Grandpa held the lids, smiled with relief and said, "Hey . . . that's a good idea"—without even realizing that he was the mastermind behind this invention. We quickly reminded him that we were merely resurrecting his genius. (I later saw this product on an "as seen on TV" commercial.)

If there's one thing I've learned and continue to learn from my grandfather—it's that in life, while we don't get to choose the cards we are dealt, we do have the choice of what we do with them. We could choose to complain that none of the cards are the same suit. We could get mad if someone else has a better hand, we could worry that we'll never get a straight or a flush—but none of these paths would lead us to a better hand of cards. All we can do is arrange our cards to the best of our ability, be mindful of what we have to work with and play an honest game. But the most important thing is to enjoy the company of who we're playing the game with. Whether it's a six-year-old or a 93-year-old, we all have a card or two to share that might just help us win the game.

MICHELLE CITRIN
Brooklyn, New York

TRANSMITTING THE SPARK

My grandmother was 16 when she married—shy, sheltered, rather plain-looking. I can just imagine her peering through her near-sighted eyes, behind thick glasses, at the broad-shouldered, red-bearded boy to whom she had been promised.

They spent their wedding night in a curtained area of her new in-laws' kitchen on the farm in Zhitomer, Ukraine, sometime around 1890. This privacy was special—the rest of the family must have sacrificed to give the newlyweds one night, alone.

When my grandmother awoke—the privilege of sleeping late would never again be hers in her entire lifetime—the family was gone. The men were in the fields; her mother-in-law was feeding the chickens.

My grandmother was hungry. It had been a night of . . . surprises. On a little side porch she found, to her delight, a small wooden bucket of sour cream and some baby cucumbers. Humming to herself, she cleaned the "pickles" and covered them with the thick cream, anticipating a good breakfast.

And a very good breakfast it might have been too. Except that in the middle of her pleasure . . . terror. In walked her mother-in-law.

"Sour cream and cucumbers, on a weekday? Foolish child! That is a breakfast to be enjoyed on a holiday, not on a working day! How were you raised—with no manners? Black bread is what we eat on an ordinary day!"

My grandmother, who had had enough trauma in the past 24 hours, burst into tears and threw herself on the bed in her tiny corner, wishing more than anything to be dead . . . or at least back home and safe with her parents and sisters and brothers.

"I don't want to be married!" she wailed.

Fortunately, my grandfather waded into the mess just at this moment. And, as the story is told, he calmed his bride, quieted his mother, salvaged the cucumbers and somehow made everything all right. It was an unusually courageous act for a man who never again had much to say in his life.

But that was the turning point for my grandmother. The lesson she learned was that tears will not save the day, or rather: "Don't cry over cucumbers and cream or anything else. It doesn't get you or your family fed."

So the shy, sheltered girl took another approach.

From deep within her, from some hidden river of resource, she pulled the strength that was needed to make her into the traditional and powerful matriarch of that generation.

She became tough, determined and capable.

It was she who persuaded my grandfather to leave the farm and move a step up, to be a peddler. It was she who, while he was peddling, set up her own shop in the village marketplace selling his rejected pots and pans at a discount, arguing and bargaining until a proper price was set.

Her babies were born and she went right back to work. Saving, scrimping, putting by. Until there were five children and enough money for tickets for all of them . . . to America!

It was she who made the plans. Steal away in the darkness. Bribe someone to take the family over the border by starlight. My father was a six-year-old and so skinny that as he crawled, belly down, under a fence, he slid right out of his pants! It was my grandmother who went back and got them. Who knows when they could afford new pants; would they even have proper pants, in America?

It was my grandmother who kept them all together on the ship. Maybe the children were afraid of her anger, or her toughness, or of a good slap. But they stayed together.

After they settled in Chicago, she kept her old habits. Save, put by, make do. Cut an apple into five pieces, one for each child. Who can afford five apples? Grandfather was still a peddler.

And from this saving came money to buy a tiny cottage with a dirt floor in the basement. This is where the family lived while the upstairs rooms were rented.

Still she scrimped. Sell the cottage, buy a two-flat. Then a six-flat. Then a huge apartment building. And a black silk dress for herself, and finally a string of pearls.

Where did it come from, this strength? This ability to set a goal and stick with it? How did this timid girl, who wept when scolded, turn into a woman who transformed her entire world?

Whatever it was—intelligence, wit, stubbornness—it is the same strength I see in her great-granddaughters and their generation. They too are in the "marketplace," selling not pots and pans but new concepts of women in new professions. They are marketing their abilities to perform any task in any arena. Unafraid of reaching out, learning new skills, trying new ideas, succeeding, sometimes falling, but always striving for new goals on distant horizons.

Many, like my grandmother, have their children and continue to work. The only difference is that these women see themselves as professionals. My grandmother was only "helping out."

It is this common thread of fearlessness that binds these two distant generations. That spark, that desire to build—burns steady and true. It is this ability to see that there is a better life out there; and it's going be theirs, no matter what it takes in determination and assertiveness.

Whether young women today are building a partnered life or a single one, a life with a career outside the home or in it, it is that pure burning flame within them that sustains.

Women like me stand with our feet in both generations. We remember our grandmothers, and we delight in our daughters. We see the link between our daughters' lives, and those of the young Jewish women of the shtetl more than a century ago.

And we bless the tough and tiny grandmothers, from many lands and cultures, who were brave enough to bring their progeny here, to grow up in a place and time where girls don't have to cry over cucumbers and sour cream.

ESTHER MANEWITH
Chicago, Illinois

HEARING A GRANDMOTHER'S VOICE

A few years ago, when I was a teenager, I fell in love with a boy who just really wasn't right for me in any way.

He was rude to my friends, but when they urged me to leave him, I didn't listen. My mom saw the way he treated me (which wasn't very good), and kept questioning why I was still with him. Her disapproval worried me, deep down, but I ignored it.

Then one day my grandmother called me and said: "Baby, what's going on with you these days? I hear that things aren't good." I knew, that moment, it was over. After her phone call, I broke off all contact with him and felt more secure in my decision than I ever thought possible.

Whenever my grandparents step into a situation involving my siblings or me, I know it must be serious and I should take notice. Let's face it: it's not the same as when a parent steps in; parents will nag you about everything and anything, but grandparents just get to be sweet to you! I know that if they are genuinely concerned about me, they must know what's best and I should listen carefully to what they have to say.

Z.H. (22)
New York, New York

THE HEART IN EXILE

Eshagh Abdollahzadeh spent the first 62 years of his life living comfortably in Tehran, buying and selling real estate, and providing heavy machinery for roadwork to sub-contractors of the Shah. A true businessman, Esi was known for his loyalty and dedication. People knew him in Iran, and they respected him.

The hardest decision of his life was uprooting his wife and children to America following the 1979 Islamic Revolution. As Jews, they were forced to seek religious asylum.

Living on Long Island, my grandmother said, "Esi suffered the way exiles suffer—he left part of his heart in Iran."

The regime took away Esi's homeland, but it did not take his sense of humor. For all the pain he felt for his beloved country, he still knew how to make his grandchildren laugh.

Friday nights at my grandparents' house were a tradition and where I hold my most precious memories with Esi. The complex aromas of traditional Persian cooking would awaken my taste buds the moment I entered the house. And the first place my eyes landed was always Esi, sitting in his old armchair and pretending to be sleeping.

"BOO!" he would shout, leaping out of his chair.

I would lunge backwards in fright, burst into laughter, then run to him, kiss him on both cheeks and give him a big hug. And then I would say: "Shabbat Shalom, Esi." Though he performed this prank every Friday night throughout my childhood and my adolescence, I had the same reaction each time.

We shared a love for my grandma's traditional Persian-style cooking. Friday night meant "Ab Goosht" (Jewish chicken soup) and "Gondi" (Persian matzoh balls), "Tadig" (Persian crispy rice) and Esi's favorite, "Khoresht Gheymeh," Persian stew with yellow peas.

"Pari, put a little *Khoresht* on my rice," he would tell my grandma. "No *Goosht* (meat)."

Esi took his health seriously and stopped eating red meat after coming to America. He never ate in restaurants, and stuck to a diet of whatever Persian food my grandmother cooked.

It was all he needed.

It tasted like home.

JESSICA KHORSANDI (20)
Great Neck, New York

Journaling Expedition #5:

Your Story and Your Family's Story in Six Words

The online storytelling site SMITH Magazine created the "Six-Word Memoir Project"® shortly after its 2005 launch, with no clue that it would become an international sensation. According to http://www.smithmag.net/sixwords:

> *Legend has it that Hemingway was once challenged to write a story in only six words. His response? "For sale: baby shoes, never worn." In November 2006, SMITH Magazine re-ignited the recountre by asking our readers for their own Six-Word Memoirs. They sent in short life stories in droves, from the bittersweet ("Cursed with cancer, blessed with friends") and poignant ("I still make coffee for two") to the inspirational ("Business school? Bah! Pop music? Hurrah") and hilarious ("I like big butts, can't lie"). Since then, the Six-Word Memoir project has become a global phenomenon and a bestselling book series . . . featured in hundreds of media outlets from NPR to The New Yorker, covered on tens of thousands of blogs, and, as of Summer 2010, can be found inside one million Honest Tea bottle caps . . .*

Readers continue to post their six-word stories on the SMITH Magazine website; and the format has been used in classrooms, churches, and synagogues, and as "icebreakers" in social, organizational, and corporate settings. It can be a deeply satisfying vehicle for processing emotions, a challenging model for self-expression, and an excellent jumping-off point for Family Meetings and discussions.

In keeping with the themes of this chapter, can you tell your (individual, personal) life story in just six words?

_____ _____ _____ _____ _____ _____

Next: How would you characterize your family unit in six words?

_____ _____ _____ _____ _____ _____

Ask your children and grandchildren for their Six-Word Memoirs about their own lives and about the family. These are wonderful statements to share and reflect on, via group emails and in person. Even the little ones in the family can participate, as long as they know how to read, write, and count! You can revisit your family's Six-Word Memoir exercise each year.

Online resources for creating Six-Word Memoirs:
http://www.smithmag.net/sixwordbook/2010/09/13/video-six-tips-for-writing-six-word-memoirs/
http://psychcentral.com/blog/archives/2011/01/06/the-story-of-your-life-in-six-words/

CHAPTER VI

THE WORLD'S OUR KITCHEN TABLE: GRAND WAYS TO STAY CONNECTED

"Everyone needs to have access to both grandparents and grandchildren in order to be a full human being."
—Margaret Mead

"You do not really understand something unless you can explain it to your grandmother."
—Unknown

Every evening, around dinnertime, Susan Sanders Witkow and her husband, Stanley, can't wait to set eyes on their adorable, red-headed granddaughter, Evie, age two, and catch up on her day. Evie clutches Big Coco, her cloth doll, and pretends to feed her, thrusting a fistful of peas at Nani Susan, who is brandishing Little Coco (the same doll, only smaller). Nani and Evie make the two Cocos dance and twirl to the tune of "You Are My Sunshine," while beaming P'pa Stanley jiggles a smiling yellow sun made out of cardboard. Sometimes they wear silly hats; sometimes they have tea parties.

Suddenly, Evie squeals, "Daddy home!" And Susan and Stanley watch her race to the front door to kiss and hug their son-in-law, followed by greetings all around.

Next comes bath time. The delighted grandparents watch Evie splash and giggle, and they chat with her about her morning at the playground with Mommy and afternoon hike with Daddy. Susan reads aloud and displays the pictures of a penguin mother and child from one of Evie's favorite books, I Like It When, *designed so that very young children can finish its sentences. And Evie does. "I like it when"* . . . *"you dance with me!" Evie calls out happily. "You kiss me g'nite!" The grandparents marvel at how new language is emerging each day and at how Evie's personality is unfolding. And they marvel too as they watch their daughter, Liz, scoop Evie out of the tub and wrap her wriggling body in a towel. Wasn't it just yesterday that that this self-assured young mother was* their *adorable little red-headed girl?*

And when it's time to say goodbye, Nani, P'pa, and Evie pucker up for lots of noisy kisses and repeated yelps of, "Bye-bye, see you tomorrow. I love you. I LOVE YOU!"

Staying Close, 21ˢᵗ-Century Style

Here's a family in which close ties between grandparents and grandchildren are a treasured tradition. Thirty years ago, when the Witkows were raising Liz and her brother, Sandy, their own parents lived very close by and participated enthusiastically in their grandchildren's lives on a daily basis.

The difference is: Susan and Stanley Witkow live in Westport, Connecticut, and their daughter and son-in-law, Liz and Ari Bader-Natal, live 3,000 miles away, in a suburb of San Francisco.

The Witkows' nightly visits with Evie and family take place via Skype. Together they sing "The Wheels on the Bus" and perform the requisite hand motions in front of their webcams—one attached to a desktop computer in Susan's home office and the other built into Liz's laptop, which rests mostly on her kitchen table, facing Evie's booster seat. When Evie clambers from her perch, Liz swivels the computer around and points the camera in whichever direction she runs.

A generation ago, chatting with children and grandchildren out of state meant being tethered to a corded telephone with costly, per-minute long-distance charges. To get face-time in real time meant that somebody had to purchase an airline ticket and take time off from work. Multiply the expenditures of time and money significantly if you or your kids lived abroad.

More Affordable, More Accessible than Ever

Not anymore, thanks to free, easily downloadable Internet-based telephone and video conferencing systems like Skype. You may already be quite familiar with this technology; you may have even been an "early adopter" of Skype when it first became available back in 2003. But according to a 2012 report from the MetLife Mature Market Institute, it's still only 12% of grandparents who have embraced it as a way of staying in touch with grandchildren. *(https://www.metlife.com/about/press-room/us-press-releases/index. html?compID=84626)*

And it's safe to say that the vast majority of grandparents who Skype are, like the Witkows, baby boomers (or even younger). No question: it's the boomers who are bridging the technology gap between their kids' generation (younger adults who grew up in a world of rapidly evolving digital communications) and their parents' generation: people my age who generally don't find these devices or operations terribly intuitive and can be intimidated by them.

But even we 75-and-overs are starting to discover that chatting via webcams, using Skype or other video communications technologies like FaceTime and Google Hangout, is, in fact, quite user-friendly for those of us who find it difficult to hunt-and-peck on a keyboard, because we never really learned how to type. Interacting "face-to-face" with our family members over a webcam can actually make conversations *easier* if our hearing isn't what it used to be. And if our vision isn't what it used to be and it's hard to see a standard-sized computer screen, Skype video can be projected on a big-screen TV. More and more assisted-living residences have webcam setups in their common spaces. According to the Pew Research Center's Internet and American Life Project (February 2012), one-third (34%) of Internet users age 65 and older use social networking sites such as Facebook; and 18% do so on a typical day. By comparison, email use continues to be the bedrock of online communications for seniors. As of August 2011, 86% of Internet users age 65 and older use email, with 48% doing so on a typical day. *(http://www.pewinternet.org/Reports/2012/Older-adults-and-internet-use.aspx)*

Susan Witkow calls this technology "a godsend." She admits that she was crushed, at first, when her daughter and son-in-law decided to settle on the West Coast, mourning the fact that she wouldn't be able to replicate her own parents' relationship with their grandchildren—taking them along on impromptu errands, hosting weekly sleepovers, and dropping in at breakfast time with favorite treats. ("My mother always brought them fresh raspberries on rye toast.") As soon as Evie was born, she promised herself she would do everything in her power to make "three thousand miles feel like three miles."

Today, it isn't only Evie who squeals with delight when the computer erupts in a familiar hum and the green "Skype" icon starts blinking. "Would it be too over the top to say that it's the reason we get up every morning?" said Susan, laughing. "Seriously, it's the highlight of our day. We stop dinner, turn off the TV, and ignore other calls. This is our time with our granddaughter."

A "Face-to-Face" Technology that Really Connects

A recent *USA Today* article ("Say Grace and Pass Grandma") supports the fact that videoconferencing can be a boon to far-flung families that make the most of them:

> *"This has always been a highly mobile society, but that high mobility, for the first time, is being counterbalanced by being able to communicate electronically—not in superficial ways but in meaningful ways," says historian Steven Mintz of the University of Texas-Austin, an expert on the history of the family. "There is a tremendous anxiety over disconnection in our modern world. We've embraced technology because*

it has allowed us to maintain in real time a connection to people we really care about."
(http://usatoday30.usatoday.com/NEWS/usaedition/2012-11-21-Thanksgiving-togetherness-when-you-cant-be-there_CV_U.htm)

During holidays, especially, family members who can't make it home can still feel connected by having a "virtual" seat at the table. They can join in saying grace, making toasts, "meeting" new babies, and oohing and aahing over the splendid-looking turkey. And everybody can greet them, in turn, and check out their surroundings in a distant city (or continent). Sure, plenty of families stay warmly in touch by phone or mail, but videoconferencing, according to *USA Today*, offers a distinct advantage:

> *"We're hungry to see people's reactions," says Richard West, a professor of communication studies at Emerson College in Boston. "We really want to be able to see whether what we're saying makes sense and is being received in the intended way."*

Changing How/When/Where We See Each Other

Plus, thanks to today's smartphones and tablets, you don't even have to be at home to videoconference. Nor do you need to live far especially from your grandkids to find the technology useful. If you spot some toddler outfits on sale at the mall, for example, you can film them and have your daughter or son give you feedback on the spot, ensuring that the size is right and that the gift will be appreciated.

Handheld media enables your grandkids to contact you, in turn, at special moments, giving you a front-row seat at their sibling's soccer game or greeting you from the Eiffel Tower during their French club's school trip, or so they can see your expression when they tell you they were just accepted by their dream college.

And should there come a day when you can't get around as well as you used to, having this technology in place will help the family look in on you.

I realize that this may be old news to some of you veteran Instagramers and Instant-Messagers. But to slow technology-adopters, it's pretty amazing stuff. So many ways, these days, to nurture The Grandest Love!

You Don't Have To Be an Expert

As excited as I've become about Skype, et al, I assure you I'm not about to launch into any detailed high-tech overviews. First of all, at the rate things are going, any cutting-edge trend I might spotlight on these pages could go the way of the eight-track tape by the time you read this book. But that's not the only reason. I admit it: demographically speaking, I'm one of those *elder*-elders for whom all this represents a "Brave New World" I haven't fully mastered. Through talking to people and writing this book, I've started learning what some of the more tech-savvy seniors are up to, and I realize I've only scratched the surface.

And I know something else: some years back, when I first started formulating my ideas for this book, I envisioned regular Family Meetings during which everybody sat around the kitchen table, writing in our notebooks about our common interests, undertaking discussions, and putting our conclusions on a whiteboard. I've had to face the fact that the nature of modern life (including, but not limited to, today's economic realities) would all too often preclude the in-person part.

The World's Your Kitchen Table

While I still love nothing more than having all my children and grandchildren under one roof, I've come to realize that communications technologies are **making the world our kitchen table,** rife with opportunities for sharing, and yes, Teaching-and-Learning. My family has wonderful interactions through our group emails about personal, philosophical, or political matters. Emailing allows all the recipients to log on and respond at an hour that works within their time zones and busy schedules. It enables everyone to digest matters, without confrontation or interruption, and to formulate thoughtful replies.

So if, for whatever reason, you've resisted jumping on the communications-technologies bandwagon, I urge you to (again) consider the importance of TRYING. If you're embarrassed or worried about a learning curve, don't let that stand in your way. I'm in pretty much the same boat! At this point, whenever I require any sort of tech support, I call on the best Teachers I know: my kids and grandkids. If no one's available, I'll get a student from our local high school (or even middle school) to come over and tackle my problem, or try and talk me through it, for a relatively modest fee. I've promised myself to make time to enroll in a computer course geared to seniors. A wide array of such courses is available in adult-education programs and community centers in practically every city and town. None are very costly; and you can even find some, mostly through seniors' organizations, that are free of charge.

Although computers have become much more affordable through the years, not everyone has the means to purchase one or to pay for an Internet connection. In that case, your best resource is your local public library, where you can log on for free. If you need help setting up a free email address, the staff can help. And then you'll be just a few keystrokes away from connecting with your grandchildren, wherever they may be living, working, or traveling.

Find Various Paths to Connect and Go with What Works

Here are a few thoughts about some other modes of communication—"ancient" and modern—that we grandparents can use to make the world our kitchen table. They don't offer the face-to-face pleasures of video-chatting; and no technology can provide the psychic benefits (for both grandparents *and* grandchildren) of a walk on the beach or a real-life hug. But even in families that live only a town or two away from each other, those precious times may be few and far between, especially as the grandkids get older.

There's no "best" way of connecting with the younger generation. Creative, flexible grandparents know they must be guided by the situation. The trick is to weave back and forth between various modes of communicating as situations warrant and as befits different family members' needs at different junctures.

Whatever seems to work best for your family: go for it! Regular interactions build bridges, in between in-person visits, where chasms might grow instead.

- **Make a realistic schedule for a regular phone-chat and don't be hurt when it doesn't happen.** Personally, I'm big on the old-fashioned telephone call. I love hearing people's voices as a window into how they're feeling. And I'm a big proponent too of just letting my grandchildren know I've had a hard day and asking them for what I call "a phone hug" . . . or offering a phone hug to them. It's much more likely that you'll actually talk to your grandchildren if you schedule a regular time. If it turns out they're too busy, don't be reproachful or give them a guilt trip; be happy they lead such active lives! Nobody likes to talk to Grandpa out of obligation, and no Grandpa should want to be talked to simply out of obligation. Be flexible; if the frequency is too much, or the times consistently don't work, readdress the schedule. For years, Ethan and I used to enjoy a phone call on Friday afternoons. Now that Ethan is in rabbinical school, that is a busy time for him to wrap up his personal and professional activities before the Jewish Sabbath begins at sundown. We moved our chats—some of them quite brief, others not—to a different day, when they can be a pleasure, not an intrusion.

- **If you don't text-message, you're missing out on what's become the leading way that today's young people like to connect.** Like it or not (and I can't say I do), text messaging

has vastly outstripped phone conversations as a way to keep in touch with the young. According to a fascinating article in the Washington Post ("Texting Generation Doesn't Share Boomers Taste for Talk," August 7, 2010), there has been a huge drop in mobile phone voice-minutes usage among younger adults and an explosion in texting. This is especially true among 18 to 24-year-olds, who, according to the Nielsen study cited in the article, averaged 1,400 texts a month. But that study was from "way back" in 2009. To give you an indication of how rapidly communications modes are changing: a similar study by the Pew Internet and American Life Project, just two years later, found that this age group exchanges "an average of 109.5 messages on a normal day"—or more than 3,200 per month! If you need to get ahold of a grandchild quickly, texting has the best chance of success. Even if they don't have a block of time to take or return a phone call, they will almost always respond immediately to a text. It's not my first choice as a way to connect, and I'm going to keep championing the old-fashioned phone call as best I can, but texting is here to stay, and it's definitely effective. And as lifelong Learners, we need to come to grips with it.
(http://pewinternet.org/Reports/2011/Cell-Phone-Texting-2011.aspx)

- **Emails are a great way to connect quickly.** The MetLife Report indicates that 31% of grandparents email these days. I often email my grandchildren thoughts I'm having about something we've talked about, or links to articles I think they'll enjoy. (An advantage of being a Teaching-and-Learning family is having more areas for sharing, because you know each other's interests.) When the grandkids are traveling outside the country, especially, email is terrific. No more waiting forever for a postcard (though they are still nice to get) or for those crinkled aerograms!

- **Social networking sites offer a window on your grandchildren's world: open it, but don't judge it.** Older adults are flocking to Facebook and photo-sharing sites (like Flickr) in droves, so they need no introduction. But

there are parameters to be observed once you get there. Grandparents.com recommends you resist the impulse to post anything or to comment on your grandchild's Facebook wall, nor should you share their photos or status updates on your wall unless you have their permission. Don't initiate "friend" requests to their friends but embrace it (and take it as a big compliment) if some of them reach out to "friend" you! You may not appreciate some of the language, photos, or declarations you see on your grandchildren's Facebook, Twitter or Instagram accounts, Tumblrs, or blogs; we older adults, for the most part, have decidedly different definitions of appropriateness and privacy. That said, if you see something that raises a red flag to you about your grandchild's wellbeing or safety, there are resources (chapter 10) how to handle it—offline. And don't overlook the Internet's other portals by which to connect. There are families that host their own web pages and reunion sites, where grandparents can participate to their hearts' content! But remember: if you regret posting something too personal, by the time you delete it, it may have already been reposted, shared, and stored by others online. When it doubt, keep it off the Internet!
(http://grandparents.about.com/od/grandparentingtoday/a/Should-Grandparents-Join-Facebook_3.htm)

- **The "ancient art" of letter writing never gets old.** I've never been much for letter writing, to be honest, but I do recognize that a handwritten note from a grandparent may become a treasured keepsake. It's a nice thing too to occasionally cut out a newspaper article that you think a grandchild will be interested in and send it in the mail. There are grandparents who regularly mail coupons to their adult children and grandchildren. I think it's nice for younger generations to experience how we used to define social networking: going to the mailbox and, among the bills and circulars, finding a real letter from a real person who loves you. Do they reciprocate? Rarely via snail mail. But they'll show their appreciation in a future phone call or email.

However You Communicate, Benefits Accrue

Before little Evie's grandparents know it, she will be busy with afterschool activities, homework, and playdates, and their Skype sessions will lessen in frequency. The Witkows are banking on the fact that today's virtual tea parties—whether or not Evie even remembers them—are building a foundation for deep and lasting connection.

Nani Susan realizes how very fortunate they are. Let's face it: not all adult children would jump for joy over a nightly Skype visit from the folks! It probably helps that her daughter and son-in-law are both enthusiastic proponents of better living through technology. Ari is a high-tech educational consultant, and Liz consults part time in social networking; she also publishes a blog (www.frecklesinthefog.com) in which she reflects on life as a young mother—another wonderful resource that enables her parents to keep abreast from afar.

But a high comfort-level with high-tech media isn't all that keeps this family connected. I found Susan's observation very telling: "I think Liz is good with it because it's how she grew up. My parents—her grandparents—laid the groundwork. They were such an intrinsic part of her childhood that it feels very natural to her to want the same thing for her own family. And actually, when I think back to my amazing grandmother—Liz's great-grandmother, the *original* 'Nani'—well, it was she who set the standard for all the warmth and closeness that has followed."

Does anyone need further proof that creating strong ties with grandchildren is "a gift that keeps on giving" for generations to come, for generations we may never see? Whether or not we received that gift ourselves, we can still give it. It's about **saying yes to TRYING,** and going the proverbial extra mile to meet our grandchildren where and how they live—whether they are across the street, across the country, or across the globe.

THE GRANDCHILDREN SPEAK

AN ELECTRONIC TREASURE-TROVE

As I look back on moments that defined my relationship with Gramps, I recall his seventieth birthday celebration, when his children and grandchildren gave him a gift that changed the way he communicated. We gave him a subscription to Prodigy, one of the early Internet service providers. He embraced the new technology and became one of the few of his generation to become Internet-proficient.

Throughout my childhood, Gramps visited frequently, and we talked on the phone almost every week. But email emerged as our most reliable form of communication. Every Friday afternoon, without fail, I received a "Shabbat Shalom" email from Gramps. And now, through the wonders of Gmail, I have a collection of more than 500 of Gramps' emails.

I have reread many of Gramps' emails over the past few days, and I am reminded of what a wonderful example he set for his grandchildren:

On *tzedekah* (the Jewish tradition of charity): "You will be pleased to learn that your brother and I will deliver food packages for Rosh Hashanah at the end of the month. He will do the driving and shlepping while I do the navigating. This is a landmark date 'cause I started doing this job with your aunt when she was 5 or 6." (8.10.10)

On devotion to one's spouse: "Today is truly a day to remember—a landmark anniversary for us! Just think—58 years of being together. I was a bashful 26 at the time. Gram was a ravishing 22. A real beauty. We were sure it was the real thing." (9.8.06)

The pleasure of life-long hobbies, including his favorite, bowling: "Gramps went wild the other night and bowled a 206. Best game of the year and I can't remember when I did as well." (5.02.08)

Consistency, however, was not his forte. The very next week, he wrote: "Bad news—bowling alley got even on the last night of the season. Tipped from a 206 to an impossible 80. Better next year, though."

I am eternally grateful to have had a role-model like Gramps, and I am extremely lucky that he left me an electronic treasure-trove of memories, advice, and Gramps-isms. I'll always remember the lessons he taught me, and my Friday evening inbox will never be the same. *(From the eulogy for Alvin "Gramps" Saper.)*

JEREMY KRESS (30)
Chicago, Illinois

GRANDPA IRA'S (VIRTUAL) BLESSING

For the past six years, I have been living and studying in Israel, thousands of miles from my family in the USA. Even so, I can say without hesitation that I have never felt closer to my Grandpa Ira (Bernstein), who is now 98. And for this I must thank a wonderful invention: video Skype.

I always had a very special connection with Grandpa, but our bond was truly forged back when I was preparing for my Bar Mitzvah. He served as my tutor and devoted countless hours to training me in the Torah readings, Hebrew prayers and synagogue rituals.

Fast-forward a dozen years, and pretty much every Friday, as the Jewish Sabbath approaches, I drop whatever I am doing in order to have a "Skype Date" with my grandfather. We talk for a significant amount of time, discussing the week that has passed, or stories from our family's history. Most importantly, I've come to truly value his wisdom and sage advice about whatever life-challenges I share with him.

When it's time to say our goodbyes, Grandpa gives me the traditional "Blessing of the Children." I bend my head slightly forward and Grandpa raises his arms as if to lay his hands upon me while he chants the holy words—just like he would if I was there in person to receive this comforting blessing.

Video Skype is a great way to stay in touch with other family members as well—and it recently came in very handy when my mom gave me a tutorial on how to roast my first chicken (while watching me bungle it).

But no exchange quite compares to seeing Grandpa's smiling face, and "feeling" his hands on me. Knowing that these are among the most important years of my life, and among the final years of his, I feel unbelievably lucky to transcend the miles and to share this weekly ritual with my grandfather.

AVI ROSENBAUM (24)
Stamford, Connecticut

OPAPA ONLINE

My Opapa Larry loved his iMac computer and relished being an octogenarian in a wired world. He started his day by logging onto his favorite news sites, and ended it with late-night games of online solitaire and poker. In between, he stayed in touch with friends and family around the globe via email, often forwarding us the semi-appropriate jokes that he and his buddies circulated. It was an enjoyable way to keep in touch. My older sister wasn't too pleased, though, when (without her permission), he emailed her ancient high-school yearbook picture to a guy he wanted to fix her up with.

I'll always remember our hilarious webcam sessions while I was in college. My floor-mates would crowd around my monitor and shout, *"What's new, Opapa?!"* (that was his trademark greeting, "SO VAHT'S NEW?") while laughing uproariously at those semi-appropriate jokes. It was hard to have much of a conversation because his hearing was pretty awful, but just by looking at him, grinning, in an old, white v-neck undershirt, you could tell that he loved the attention from all the cute girls.

When he passed away at age 84 a few years ago, those girls were hugely supportive to my family and me, because Opapa had become a real person to them.

If he'd lived a little longer, I'm positive he would have joined Facebook and have had a ball with it—updating constantly, posting political articles and silly cartoons, "liking" like crazy and friending everyone he met. Young people often don't appreciate being indiscriminately friended by older folks. But Opapa was such a character, I doubt anybody would have minded. I don't even want to *think* about the stuff he might have Tweeted.

Miss you a lot, Lorbeer18@aol-dot-com!

ARIELLE O.S. (24)
Wilton, Connecticut

Journaling Expedition #6:

Plugged and Unplugged

1. **"Yesterday."** While this chapter enthusiastically embraces the advantages of living in a wired world, some things are lost when you are "plugged in" 24/7. Do you have any memorable experiences or thoughts to share that will give your grandchildren a picture of what it was like to be young in a world without mobile phones, personal computers, or Internet?

_____

_____

_____

_____

_____

2. **"Today."** Having regular contact with adult children and grandchildren is more likely to occur if together you come up with a realistic plan that takes everyone's needs, desires, and schedules into account. Make some notes on what your own hopes and wishes are for when and how often you will get together, call, or video-chat, and find out what works for your family members.

_____

_____

_____

_____

_____

3. **"Tomorrow."** Whether you're an early adopter or someone who needs help programming your phone, there are always new things to learn. Keep an ongoing wish-list of technology skills you'd like to master, products you'd like to own, or services you're interested in trying. Maybe your family members or some young people in your neighborhood will be willing to provide tech support to help you get started.

_____

_____

_____

_____

CHAPTER VII

MAKING GRAND MEMORIES: TEACHING AND LEARNING, LIVING AND LOVING

"To show a child what has once delighted you, to find the child's delight added to your own, so that there is now a double delight seen in the glow of trust and affection, this is happiness."

—J. B. Priestley

"Can't find it in Miss Manners' book
But I've a hunch
You should leave a very big tip cool
When you take a toddler to lunch."
—Howard Eisenberg
("Toddler Empire" poems,
www.grandparents.com)

On Making Memories: A Meditation

As older adults, we sometimes feel as if we've seen and done it all; there is little that surprises us anymore. An awareness of loss, of time growing shorter, may preoccupy us.

But The Grandest Love takes us to an oasis in time and space, an oasis where promise—not loss—reigns. No question: there's a bit of magic about it. As harried and uncertain as life can be nowadays—in this place, the days are sweeter, gentler, and filled with amazement and delight even if it's been a very long time since you were thoroughly amazed or delighted.

This place, this moment in time, is the intersection where grandparents and grandchildren meet. If you're already there, you know what I'm talking about. If not, get ready to marvel and to make the most of it.

Of course, even in this land of sweetness, the terrain isn't perfect. But The Grandest Love has a way of making things work out. Some fortunate grandparents can still play a mean game of tennis with their grandkids. Others will cuddle on the couch and play gin rummy. Taking a grandchild to Paris? Fabulous, if you are in good-enough health and can afford pricey vacations. Creating a Project-Runway-style fashion show on the "runway" of your living-room rug? Priceless.

Your pint-sized fellow travelers look up to you, literally and figuratively. One day, they won't be little anymore and will be occupied with pursuits and (unfortunately) pressures of their own. But you'll always have Paris, or that living room—and above all, their deep and abiding trust.

That trust is what will come—I promise you—from reading and singing and drawing together, from drinking the rain, eating ice cream before dinner *(shhh . . . don't tell!)*, catching frogs, growing herbs; making paper airplanes and collages, spaghetti and messes. Go on: climb into the Batmobile—you're Batman, and he/she's Robin! Compose an email to the president of the United States. Paint each other's nails, each nail a different color. Introduce a five-year-old to Woody Woodpecker, a 15-year-old to Woody Allen. Get tips from a 10-year-old on how to play games on your iPhone.

Party Like It's 1999

What a gift to be able to recycle the old punchlines, favorite ditties, and classic family stories (happy ones/sad ones) to an unjaded audience that hangs on your every word, just as you will hang on *theirs*. Because there's a good chance that—today or in a distant tomorrow—they will open up to you about God and parents, friends and teachers, secrets and dreams, in a way that they might not to anyone else.

The Grandest Love blossoms perennially in a judgment-free zone. How rare it is to love and to be loved unconditionally. All in a circle of respectful sharing and respectful listening, good Teaching and good Learning, continuous giving and continuous getting.

An Abundance of Resources

When I first contemplated a chapter about making memories with grandchildren, my research indicated that there is no shortage of "how-to" books, websites, and articles for grandparents in search of imaginative, affordable ways to have fun with their grandchildren. By typing a few key words into a search engine, you can track down creative ideas for projects and activities, and kid-friendly excursions, complete with current web addresses and updated details. Because information becomes obsolete so quickly these days, I'm listing only a few of today's leading resources at the end of this chapter.

My research underscored another point: this is a wonderful time in history to be a grandparent! One of the key reasons is that there is strength in numbers, something that should come as no surprise to baby boomers. In May 2012, the popular website Grandparents.com (an excellent clearinghouse for information, advice, and ideas) issued a press release chronicling its growth:

> The "Ultimate Resource for Grandparents" and a premier social media website for Americans over 50 announced a 25% increase in the number of website members in April 2012, an

increase of 100,000 new members. Total membership now exceeds 500,000 members . . . with over 6,000,000 unique annual website visitors.

Jeffery Mahl, President of Grandparents.com, added: "Grandparents are increasingly engaging with our brand and valuing the exceptional features, benefits, products and services we are bringing to them through our wide network of Marketing Partners and Affiliates across Entertainment, Travel, Shopping, Dining, Insurance, Wellness, Financial Services and other sectors . . . It is a testament to our success in executing on our aggressive business expansion model . . . The website offers enriching activities, discussion groups, expert advice, ten monthly newsletters, and a Benefits Club with discounts on thousands of goods and services. In 2011, Grandparents.com added over 200 marketing partners to its Benefits Club and launched the Grandparents.com Bookstore."

Leave it to the graying boomers, my own children and their cohorts, to transform grandparenting into the coolest, hottest, "next big thing."

It's the Little Things

In the spirit of "write what you know," I'll be the first to admit I know very little, for example, about the "how-to" of crafts projects that kids will enjoy. (That was my late wife's department, and she was splendid at it.) What I do know is the WHY: *why* it is so very important that we find **a mutually enjoyable entry-point for connecting with each grandchild** — through sewing a Halloween costume together or playing catch, going to the ice-cream store or watching a movie on TV, or even just having our own silly nicknames or private jokes. Child development experts have long declared that, in the life of a youngster, these sorts of activities are neither simple nor silly. They are, in fact, the building blocks of learning, growth, confidence, and connection. **And all of them are key to the development of what has emerged as a chief predictor of**

life satisfaction and success: resilience, how one deals with adversity.

The American Academy of Pediatrics has released what they call "The Seven C's of Resilience." And they assert that what greatly fosters resilience is a support system—the proverbial village—that makes children and adolescents feel secure, heard, and loved. I can't think of anything more valuable we can do for our grandchildren than to be part of the village that fosters these "Seven C's":

Competence—the ability to handle situations effectively.

Confidence—the solid belief in one's own abilities.

Connection—close ties to family, friends, school, and community give children a sense of security and values that prevent them from seeking destructive alternatives to love and attention.

Character—a fundamental sense of right and wrong that helps children make wise choices, contribute to the world, and become stable adults.

Contribution—when children realize that the world is a better place because they are in it, they will take actions and make choices that improve the world. They will also develop a sense of purpose to carry them through future challenges.

Coping—children who learn to cope effectively with stress are better prepared to overcome life's challenges.

Control—when children realize that they can control their decisions and actions, they're more likely to know that they have what it takes to bounce back.

(Excerpted from the AAP Patient Education brochure, "Helping Your Child Cope With Life," ©2006 American Academy of Pediatrics.)

A youngster can't be lectured or prodded to adopt the Seven C's. These traits are byproducts of Teaching-and-Learning, giving and taking, laughing and loving. They are a byproduct, too, of our grandchildren watching how we live, how we treat each other, and how we pick ourselves up when we stumble.

They are a byproduct of the stories we tell about our lives and the words we use to tell them.

A Family's Unique Vocabulary

I've often felt that there's something wonderful about families that pepper their conversations with a special vocabulary all their own. Shared experiences create shared memories, often giving rise to a unique, intimate "family language." These telegraphic little messages and mottos sometimes link several generations of treasured family lore. Here are a few that people shared with us:

"Grandma Bessie did it!"

Our very elderly grandmother lived in our home when we were growing up during the 1950s. Whenever our parents got irritated with us and demanded that the culprit come forward ("Who left that bike in the middle of the driveway?" "Who took my scissors?"), my brother and I invariably replied, "GRANDMA BESSIE!" More often than not, it made them smile because our lies were so ridiculously transparent.

After Grandma Bessie died, we continued to blame her for everything from unflushed toilets to mislaid keys and lost TV remotes. In the ensuing years, we bequeathed the legend of Grandma Bessie to our children, who would use it as a buzzword to defuse our anger, usually disproportionate, about missing household objects or minor mischief.

The legend continues. Recently, my six-year-old granddaughter declared (with a wicked twinkle in her eye) that the sticky fingerprints all over my iPad after she played with it, had been left by none other than "Grandma Bethie."

"Good Luck with That . . ."

Whenever anyone (especially his children) would approach my late Uncle Jack with a plan he considered ill-advised—and his judgment was unerringly accurate—he would always offer the same wry response: "Good luck with that." He never tried to push his solutions on people, only hinted, via that pithy statement, that they would do well to think things through more fully.

Today, many years later, his children and grandchildren all know that when someone in the family gives you a quizzical look and says "good luck with that," it means your idea sounds half-baked and probably needs work.

"Silky!"

Gramps loved telling us stories about his beloved collie, Silky. She was his childhood pet during the 1930s, so none of us grandkids had ever even laid eyes on her. Nonetheless, throughout our own childhoods, whenever my sisters and I spotted a collie, we'd get very excited and point to it, shouting, "Silky, Silky!"

When we all became parents ourselves, we shared the tales of our grandfather's brave, smart, beautiful dog with our own children; and—to the puzzlement of onlookers—our entire extended family to this day continues to refer to the breed as "Silkies."

It just makes us happy.

Have I bequeathed a motto to the Witkovsky family? According to the grandkids (chapter 10), it's this: **"Always leave your campsite better than you found it."** Through the years, this has come to have a much deeper meaning than the admonition of a long-ago camp director (me) about picking up trash, not disturbing the environment, and leaving the grounds in excellent condition for the next people who will want to enjoy them. It's about actively becoming a caring citizen of the world, who leaves it a better place than when you came aboard. It's my hope that each of my grandchildren, in his or her utterly unique way, will strive to do just that in one form or another. And that I will have helped them do so in some small way—like the grandparents who are fondly remembered in the charming stories above, and below.

THE GRANDCHILDREN SPEAK

LIFE ON THE FARM

My grandma Nettie was an old-fashioned Midwestern farm wife. She and Grandpa had nine children whom they raised on a rented farm in central Illinois. I was her first grandchild, and I always felt I was her favorite, though many others came after me.

I was a premature baby, and they say I had constant colic. My inexperienced parents didn't know how to cope with it, so they asked Grandma to take care of me. Whatever she did, it worked; I guess that was when we first bonded.

From the time I was a young child, in the 1940s, I started spending summers with my grandparents. Four of my aunts and uncles still lived at home on the farm; my parents and I lived about 100 miles away, so this was a real adventure for me. They had electricity, but no running water and few other modern conveniences.

Grandma baked bread every other day, and always made a muffin-sized, miniature loaf just for me. She let me help her knead the bread, and sometimes with the pies she baked for Sundays.

On Saturdays, we went into town to do the weekly grocery shopping at the local Red & White store. Occasionally, they would buy cattle-feed, which came in brightly patterned calico sacks; she would let me pick out the ones I liked best, and then use the material to make me a dress and matching bonnet. (She tried to teach me how to sew, but I never did catch on to it.)

She used to play an old organ that she had to pump with her feet, and we sang gospel songs from an old hymnal.

Saturdays were bath-time and hair-washing time. Bathwater from the pump was heated on the woodstove, and I was allowed to be the first to sink into the tin circular tub. (I think she used the same bathwater for herself.) She washed my hair outside on the porch, using a pitcher of water and a washbasin, and a beaten egg for shampoo.

She taught me so many things: important skills like cooking and baking, gardening and canning. Some of the skills didn't end up being that important, in my life—like how to sneak an egg from under a sitting hen who was guarding her nest. But most of all, she instilled in me patience, kindness, and faith.

I owe her so much.

BARBARA HOWARD (80)
Naples, Florida

CHOCOLATE, A WORLD AWAY

My grandfather spoke some English, but not much. I speak some Hindi, but not much. But we both loved chocolate.

When I would visit him in New Delhi once a year, we made it a ritual to buy a bag of chocolate and just sit together—sometimes in silence, sometimes engaging in halting small talk. It was peaceful. Joyous.

At times I felt like I was missing out; he wasn't the sort of grandfather who I could sit and talk to for hours, who gave me sage advice on life and love. All we did was eat sweets and watch television.

Since he passed away, though, I can never eat a piece of chocolate without thinking about him and his smile. Those moments mean the most to me today. I would do anything to be with him, enjoying a Hershey's Kiss.

PRIYA VIJ (21)
Houston, Texas

WEDNESDAYS

Every Wednesday afternoon, my grandparents came to pick me up from elementary school. They would enter the playground arm in arm—"Boomar" in her white sunhat and "Popeye" in his Lacoste sweater-vest with the little green crocodile. (I guess the first grandchild really does determine what we call our grandparents; my oldest brother thought our grandfather resembled the cartoon sailor, and "Boomar" was how he mangled the word "Grandma" as a toddler.)

Boomar and Popeye, like most grandparents who live near their grandkids, came to all the special events like dance recitals, graduations, and birthday parties. But this was not a special event; this was Wednesday afternoon. After we left the schoolyard, we headed to McDonald's. In the car I would tell them about my day, and they would tell me stories, sing songs, or make jokes.

When we got to McDonald's the routine was always the same: Popeye ordered while Boomar and I picked out a booth in the back. I watched as she scrupulously cleaned off the table and laid out the silverware. I, of course, always ordered a Happy Meal (to get the toy *du jour*); the two of them ordered burgers, coffee, and a gooey little apple pie that came in a red box. If I ate all my dinner, Popeye would always give me a bite of their pie as a treat.

Some years later, long after they had both passed, I was alone traveling through an airport in a foreign country. I was a little homesick and a little hungry, and a lot confused—mostly because I did not speak the language. While waiting for my flight, I noticed a McDonald's, so I walked in and ordered an apple pie. Okay, it was not some authentic local cuisine or a gourmet delicacy—but that pastry in the red box was the best apple pie I ever had.

It tasted like home, and it reminded me of love, and of Wednesday afternoons.

COLEEN QUIGLEY (23)
Rockville Centre, New York

THE LITTLE QUEEN

When my brother was born in the 1950s, my father would bring me to my grandparent's house every morning, so my mother would have time with the new baby. I was treated like the little queen at my Nona and Pappoo's home. As my grandfather, whom I adored, said his morning prayers, I would follow him around and say "Amen, Amen!"

After he left for work, I helped my grandmother and great-grandmother as they cleaned up, cooked and baked. They gave me small things to do to help out. In that warm kitchen I learned about my religion, how to cook, clean and bake, but even more important, I learned about giving and returning unconditional love.

IRENE BURSTEIN (65)
Sherman Oaks, California

CRUISIN' WITH GRANNY

They say you never really know a person until you've traveled with them. Well, I'm here to say that this is true—even when that person is your Granny.

My grandmother, Sarah Doppelt, had always dreamed of visiting Russia (where her family hailed from), but my Grandpa Jack was too frail in his final years to undertake the journey. In 2011, Granny learned about a 12-day river cruise from Moscow to St. Petersburg, and asked me to be her travel companion. It didn't take me long to say yes.

Having grown up in the same town where our maternal grandparents lived, my brother and I were always very close with them; our childhoods were filled with Friday-night sleepovers at their house, extended-family vacations, and going to Giants games together. A few years ago, after graduating from college, I even lived in Granny's two-bedroom condo for a couple of months before finding my own place. But a 25-year-old guy sharing a tiny cabin on a cruise ship with his 85-year-old grandmother??

Believe me, I got plenty of teasing about this, along with a few raised eyebrows. Still, I knew that Granny and I always had fun together. I also knew I couldn't afford such a trip on my own, and I doubted she would go by herself. I decided it was an experience I couldn't pass up.

"Travels with Granny" turned out to be an experience, all right—and the fascinating history of Russia, its beautiful vistas and landmarks, was only part of it. While our 250 fellow passengers were mostly an older crowd, Granny was actually the oldest person on the ship—and I was the youngest by far. We were definitely "the odd couple," sitting next to each other on every bus-ride and at every meal, at the circus and at the ballet, and walking the cobblestoned streets with Granny's arm firmly clenching mine. (The woman has an AMAZING amount of energy.) A lot of the other passengers clamored to eat dinner with us because they were intrigued by our relationship. And everybody had something to say about it—from "I hope when my granddaughter is old enough, we'll travel together like the two of you!" to "MY rotten grandson would never go on a cruise with me—he won't even go to a movie with me!"

Of course, we had our moments. Granny routinely accosted people and asked them to take our picture in front of every landmark in Russia. And while the amenities on board were, in fact, sub-par, I found myself rolling my eyes as Granny (who is very particular about her food), along with the other senior citizens, complained nonstop at every meal. (I'm sure I drove her a little nuts too sometimes!)

Still, we had a great time—and leave it to Granny to make lemonade out of any lemon. After we got back, she wrote a strong letter to the tour operator, detailing her displeasure. Believe it or not, they offered her a free 12-day cruise on the Rhine.

And believe it or not: I recently returned from cruise number two, with my number-one travel companion. Once again, we had a ball.

It takes a bit of compromising from both parties to make it work, but I highly recommend that grandparents invite grandkids to travel with them, and that grandkids go for it. Our travels brought Granny and me closer than ever and created wonderful memories. And thanks to her, I've got photographs of every single one of them.

DANIEL NEGRIN (26)
Livingston, New Jersey

MY FAVORITE RELATIVE, GEE

Gee is my mother's father or my grandfather. He is called that because when my older cousin was born he couldn't say grandpa so it came out Gee. He was called that ever since.

Gee lives with my grandmother in Greenacres, Florida. I like the place my grandfather lives because we can play outside, go swimming, and take walks together. Since there aren't many kids around, we play together. Sometimes in the pool I get on his back, he shoves off, and I get off. Then we both laugh really hard and I swallow water.

Sometimes I help him in his shop. Sometimes we make earrings. Other times we make refrigerator magnets. Once I helped remake a whole sign.

What I like best about him is his sense of humor. Sometimes we just watch a funny video or something.

I love my grandfather because of who he is.

NOAH SCHNOLL
(26, written at age 7)
Richmond, Virginia

THE COUNTER AT WOOLWORTH'S

Now that I'm a grandfather myself, I realize it is the simple things that create indelible memories for grandchildren. I remember one Saturday when I was five or six years old, my Grandma Rosie took me downtown on the old Red Car streetcar line, to the grand old Los Angeles Theater—a film palace the likes of which I had never seen—to see a Dean Martin and Jerry Lewis movie.

Afterwards we went to lunch and sat at the counter at Woolworth's. I had grilled cheese and a chocolate shake.

This is still my favorite diner meal.

STANLEY WITKOW (65)
Westport, Connecticut

PASSING ON YOUR TALENTS

Abuelo, you're a true "Renaissance Man": you paint, you draw, you play soccer and watch soccer, you listen to classical music and even write some; you speak Spanish, English and Hebrew. You're the only grandfather I know who runs marathons and half-marathons. You taught me about coin collections and have every Israeli stamp ever made.

Coolest of all, you have tapes of all the Argentina World Cup games for me to watch . . . AND you are passing on all of your talents to ME.

JORDAN S.
(Pelham Jewish Center HS)
Pelham, New York

PLANTING THE MARIGOLDS

I was the firstborn of parents who grew up around the corner from each other in the Clason Point section of the Bronx—an Irish-Catholic neighborhood that teemed with children and with my aunts, uncles and cousins.

Mom's parents had eight children. By the time I came along in 1947, I was their twentieth grandchild, so I didn't represent anything new or exciting. Grandpa Jordan was "happy-go-lucky"—meaning, he was usually drinking and only occasionally a working man. I remember him packing tobacco into his pipe and watching the ballgame, or sitting in a chair in his garden, watching his vegetables grow. He taught me how to eat a plum tomato right out of the ground: first suck it clean and then add a sprinkle of salt, which he kept handy in the garden! He was right— those tomatoes were delicious when they were warm from the sun.

To my *paternal* grandparents, however, I was a gift—the first grandchild *and* a girl, which was very exciting because they had three sons (all recently returned from the war). They doted on me, and Grandma McLaughlin told me I was beautiful every chance she got. Grandma mostly stayed home and prepared meals; it was not a time during which gender roles were examined too closely. It was Grandpa McLaughlin who taught me life's grand lessons, in small increments—about work, responsibility, community and play.

Grandpa sold insurance for Prudential. Whenever I—and later, my brothers—would visit, he'd let us play with the typewriter, rubber stamps and spinning desk-chair in his home office. After going door-to-door to collect very small premiums from his clients, he would sit at the dining room table and sort the bills. He taught me to put them in order of value, to line them up (all facing the same way), to count them twice, and then to fill out the deposit slips. Then we'd go to the bank, where he'd introduce me to all the tellers.

Grandpa would take me to Gansey's Saloon, where I was allowed to order a Shirley Temple but could sit only at a table, not at the bar. While he drank his beer, the bartender would fill up a quart jar for him to take home. Afterwards we often stopped at the pickle-packer next door and buy a quart of pickles and sometimes olives or pickled onions. Here too he would introduce me; I don't remember anyone else ever introducing me to adults, as a child.

I loved it when Grandpa would leave his coat-and-tie at home—I don't think he ever owned a pair of jeans, work-pants or shorts—and take us to the beach to fly a kite. He taught us how to make a tail for the kite from old rags, to RUN to get the kite in the air, and how to hold it so it stayed up there. He often took us to the Bronx Zoo. We loved the adventure of riding in his fancy sky-blue Buick and getting to decide which way to drive there and what to see after we got there. It remains one of my favorite destinations.

Best of all was when he taught me to garden. He let me dig up the dirt to loosen it and then use my fingers to create two rows, and spread the marigold seeds as if I was sprinkling gold dust. *Cover it up, pat it down and check on it every time you come to visit.* Those were my marigolds. The other gardening chore was to trim the dead roses off the bushes that climbed up the wall of the garage. He let me do this all by myself!

And every morning he'd go out to the garden and cut a rose to wear in his lapel.

On very special occasions, we were allowed to spend the night at Grandma and Grandpa McLaughlin's. This was a huge treat because we got to sleep in the convertible sofa in the living room—in front of the television. We begged to be allowed to get into bed as soon as dinner was over. The best nights were the Saturdays when we watched the fights and got to root for the black trunks or the white trunks. (I did not retain my love of boxing.)

Today I am a grandmother of four, ages six to ten. They are growing up quickly. Technology makes them accessible even though they are thousands of miles away. They have so many more diversions than I had at their age—I'm not sure they would be enthralled by my memories of the marigolds. They like to perform shows for us when all they're all together and have me take pictures of their antics. The next time they come over, they count the framed photos I display throughout the house, to see who has the most! They enjoy when we do art projects with my "grown-up" paints, tools, and techniques. They also like teaching me their latest Wii games, and how to do new things (like play games) on my iPad and phone.

When I visit them, I have them take me on a tour of their classrooms and to meet their teachers. For a long-distance grandparent, a tour of their home turf provides genuine insight into their world. I find that their lessons are more sophisticated and self-taught than in my day. I've learned they know much more than I'd assumed.

Grandparenting is marigold seeds, kites and zoos; it is pictures, school events and gymnastics performances. But really, it is so much more than that. Hopefully I will leave my grandchildren the gift of feeling loved and confident, and of caring about the world beyond themselves. And the gift of good memories, as I have, fifty years hence.

DENISE MCLAUGHLIN (62)
New Canaan, Connecticut

LEARNING FROM THE GENERATIONS BEFORE US

It seems like yesterday that I was the little girl staying over at Grandma's house, looking through her desk drawer and finding treasures. Now I collect Social Security and have four beautiful grandchildren of my own. In between, I raised three sons, who got to spend time with four wonderful grandparents. We're blessed that my folks are still here too.

My grandpa loved to take us fishing; my dad was always in his glory taking the kids to a 7-Eleven to buy a treat. My husband learned to be a "supergrandpa" from my dad. Regardless of how we express it, this is how we learn to be grandparents: from the special people who took time to be there for us.

I only hope to be able to enjoy each moment—the birthdays, and camp shows, the spontaneous hugs. It takes proximity, making sure the moments happen, and lots of love.

MARTHA KAPLAN BACKER

I ♥ MY SURROGATE GRANDMOTHERS!

I have a great family, but there's one thing I never had: a grandmother. My Grandma Carol (my mother's mother) died before I was born, and Omama Ruth (my dad's) died only a few months after.

My parents and I assumed that this would always be a big void in my life, but we were wrong. Two great ladies have filled that void in a very special way. Both of them have "real" grandchildren, whom they love—and they also have big hearts, with plenty of room for ME.

Tante Judy was my Grandma Carol's best friend from college. Throughout my childhood, she took me to see *The Nutcracker* every winter. I can't even count how many ballets I've seen with her at Lincoln Center. Afterwards we walk back to her apartment, she grills salmon for me the way I like it, and we talk for hours. The night before the Macy's Thanksgiving Day Parade, we watch the huge balloon characters get blown up in her neighborhood. Her lemon squares are the best in the world, and I've always had a great time baking them with her during sleepovers.

My other "surrogate" grandmother is Grandma Sarah. (Her late husband, Jack, was Omama Ruth's cousin.) Sarah is one of the most optimistic people I know. Even in her late eighties she can walk miles and never complains; she does everything with a big smile. She even came to Disneyland with my family! We have so much fun shopping together and going to movies. I love to talk with her and I especially like hearing stories about when she and Jack fell in love and got married, many years ago.

These two women do everything for me that a grandmother would do and I know they are always there for me. They are both beautiful and amazing and I love them so much. I know they are proud of my accomplishments.

I think it would be great if *more* older people looked around to see whether there's a kid they could "adopt" as their grandchild. Take it from me: we make each other very happy!

RACHEL CLAIRE ORBACH (14)
New York, New York

A MODEL TRAIN AND A WALK AFTER DINNER

I'm extremely fortunate to have a grandfather who, at almost 97, is still healthy and spry! For birthdays and anniversaries, he writes poems from the heart that incorporate much wisdom about what makes the recipient special.

I have the honor of housing an amazing model train-track that he spent many, many hours building. As a child I learned how to be gentle with it, and loved watching him patiently construct it. Now my kids love talking with him about trains, baseball, and what life was like when he was young.

When I was little we'd take special walks after dinner—just the two of us. I loved walking with him and talking about life. My husband and I try to do this with our kids whenever possible—it's a great way to end the day!

ROBIN (41)
Chicago, Illinois

Journaling Expedition #7:

Making Memories: A Shared Expedition with Grandchildren

1. If you already have grandchildren, what are some of the memorable experiences/moments you've shared, and what made them special? Now ask the grandkids that question and see how their answers differ or are the same (from yours, and each other's).

_____

_____

_____

_____

_____

2. Does your family have a shared vocabulary (i.e., buzzwords, nicknames)? What are they, and what are the stories behind them? Ask your grandchildren the same question. It will be fun to talk about how the words got started!

_____

_____

_____

_____

_____

3. *"Let's Go and Do!"* Make a wish-list of things you'd love to do you're your grandchildren someday, and why you think it would be wonderful. Have them do the same thing and see how they match. What would it take to have these experiences come to fruition? Is this something you should be planning for?

_____

_____

_____

_____

_____

Resources for Activities with Grandchildren:

We cannot vouch for all their contents, but these popular sites and books seemed to have real appeal and staying power. And most offer a good deal more than creative ideas, projects, and games.

- www.grandparents.com
- www.aarp.org
- www.grandmagazine.com
- Elderhostel ("the not-for-profit world leader in lifelong learning") offers international educational/travel adventures specially geared to grandparents and grandchildren: www.roadscholar.org/programs/grandparenttravel.asp
- *GrandLoving; Making Memories with Your Granchildren* by Sue Johnson, Julie Carlson, and Elizabeth Bower. And the website www.grandloving.com
- *Super Granny: Great Stuff to Do with Your Grandkids,* by Sally Wendkos Olds
- *To Our Children's Children: Preserving Family Histories for Generations to Come,* by Bob Greene and D.G. Fulford
- *The Family StoryHandbook: How to Use Stories, Anecdotes, Rhymes, Handkerchiefs, Paper and Other Objects to Enrich Your Family Traditions,* by Anne Pellowski

CHAPTER VIII

A GRAND EXPEDITION: CREATING A LIVING LEGACY

"Everyone must leave something behind when he dies, my grandfather said. A child or a book or a painting or a house or a wall built or a pair of shoes made. Or a garden planted. Something your hand touched some way so your soul has somewhere to go when you die, and when people look at that tree or that flower you planted, you're there. It doesn't matter what you do, he said, so long as you change something from the way it was before you touched it into something that's like you after you take your hands away."
　　　　　　　　　　　　　　　—Ray Bradbury (*Fahrenheit 451*)

"If you know when you have enough you are wealthy,
If you carry your intentions to completion you are resolute,
If you live a long and creative life, you will leave an eternal legacy."
　　　　　　　　　　　　　　　—Lao Tzu

"What will I leave behind in this world? What will be my legacy?"

Through the many years that I've been listening to grandparents share their hopes and dreams, their regrets and fears, the word "legacy" is one that comes up over and over. It's a word that carries much weight and many meanings. Most of us, of course, are concerned about our legacy in its most tangible manifestation: a financial bequest or endowment. Regardless of our financial bracket, we hope to maximize whatever we may be able to pass down to our heirs.

The Grandest Love bespeaks an investment in grandchildren's lives that goes beyond money. We hope that, in some way, the deepest principles that have guided our own lives will be carried forth by them as they forge their unique paths into the future.

I'm sure I didn't coin this phrase, but it captures the idea beautifully: **we want to leave *values*, not only *valuables*.**

And in this chapter, I'm going to give you some ideas on how you can "bequeath" both values and valuables while you're still around to enjoy it by working with your grandchildren to devise your own family's **"Living Legacy Foundation."**

Values and Valuables

But first let's explore what a legacy may mean. Once again, I turn to author Stephen R. Covey:

> *There are certain things that are fundamental to human fulfillment. The essence of these needs is captured in the phrase "to live, to love, to learn, to leave a legacy." The need to live is our physical need for such things as food, clothing, shelter, economical well-being, health. The need to love is our social need to relate to other people, to belong, to love and to be loved. The need to learn is our mental need to develop and to grow. And the need to leave a legacy is our spiritual need to have a sense of meaning, purpose, personal congruence, and contribution. (The 7 Habits of Highly Effective People, 1989)*

When it comes to values, are there any guarantees that our grandchildren will actually embrace our legacy? Will they proudly transmit our cultural or religious heritage? Will they treasure our Bubbie's handwritten recipe book from the old country? Will they teach their own children to love the Chicago Cubs? The reality is, there are no guarantees of any of it. Here's the best we can do, the best we should hope for:

- That through ongoing Teaching-and-Learning, throughout our lifetime, and by the example of how we've lived each day, **our grandchildren will know what our values are and why they matter to us so deeply;** and even if they don't share all of these values or even agree with them, they will respect them.

- That they will **grow into people of strong morals, passions, family-feeling, and convictions**—the kinds of people who will strive to leave behind their own meaningful legacies.

Naturally, in thinking about our legacy to our grandchildren, we must never ignore the powerful influence of the generation in-between—our adult children—and the fact that the beliefs and values they wish to instill in their offspring rightfully take precedence over ours. We all know that adult children sometimes take paths that strongly diverge from how we raised them. It is terribly important never to undermine or criticize their way of life through our words or actions. I don't underestimate how difficult such situations can be, especially in regard to (for example) religious differences, when one generation or the other is extremely devout. **Yet in all faiths and belief systems, "peace in the family, harmony in the home" is a core value. For us, as family elders, to steadfastly uphold this principle may be the most important legacy we can leave.**

Introducing: The Living Legacy Foundation

During my many heartfelt discussions with grandparents about their legacies (financial and otherwise), something always nagged at me. Virtually all those discussions began with somebody declaring solemnly, **"After I die . . ."** as the preamble to their ideas. This was the case whether the grandparent was 55 or 85—or rich or poor, or anywhere between. I asked myself:

Why do we have to be dead before the fruits of our labors can be put to good use? Why can't we savor the outcomes and experiences together with our heirs?

And that's what sparked the idea that grew into the **Witkovsky Living Legacy Foundation.** It's been such a rewarding undertaking for our family that I'm sharing the nuts-and-bolts with you as a guide, should you wish to create a "Living Legacy" suited to your family's unique relationships, needs, and goals.

For starters: a Living Legacy Foundation, as we've devised it, is not a "family foundation" in the usual sense. Its "board of directors" and its beneficiaries are one and the same: they're the grandchildren (ages 13 and up). The grandchildren propose the projects or purchases they are interested in, and I provide the funding; but how (or if) the monies are allocated—who gets how much—is strictly for them to decide together, by and for themselves.

It's important to note that before inaugurating this venture, I carefully reviewed it with my daughter and son and their spouses to get their input and make sure they were on board. If, for whatever reason, they were not in favor of it, I wanted to respect the primacy of *their* wishes for *their* children. (Plus, I wanted to assure them that they were under no obligation to contribute to or to take over the funding at any juncture.)

Let me also point out that you do not need to be a Grand-Daddy Warbucks to get a Living Legacy Foundation off the ground; I'm surely not one! Even a relatively modest fund of several hundred dollars can provide a meaningful and extremely satisfying experience for all. (Of course, the more dollars you are willing or able to invest, the more significant proposals you can underwrite.)

So here's how it works:

- Your grandchild identifies an activity (a travel experience, a course or enrichment program) or a purchase (equipment, materials, etc.) that relates to her education, her career, one of her major interests, passions, or goals—or an avenue she is very curious to explore further. *(I'll stick with the female pronoun, here, for expediency.)*

- **She then submits a short, simple "request for funding" to the board, i.e., her siblings and cousins.** Her request should provide a brief overview of the proposed project/activity/purchase ("P/A/P"), including what interests her most about it and what the associated costs are, what percentage she is asking the foundation to underwrite, and how she plans to cover the remainder (if applicable). The request may be made in the form of an informal email, or by filling out and scanning the short form on the next page.

- **The proposals are reviewed and voted on via email or by phone, unless the timing coincides with a holiday or family celebration, and they can get together in person.** In that case, the board convenes behind closed doors until they reach a unanimous decision to fund the proposal, to fund it partially or not to at all. (And boy, do I love hearing the muffled sounds of laughter and lively debate wafting through the house! This says to me that creative ideas are being shared, relationships are being cemented, and responsible approaches to finances are being inculcated—an infinitely more valuable Teaching-and-Learning experience than Grandpa simply handing over a check!)

- **As in any granting process, there is follow-up.** Each Living Legacy Fund recipient is expected to report back on their experiences, be it through a travel journal or photos, or whichever way they can create a learning experience for the rest of the family.

One Family's "Living Legacy" Projects

The Witkovsky family's Living Legacy Foundation contributed toward Ethan's tuition when the scholarship funds at his rabbinical school were suddenly cut. It paid for Benny to journey to the United States-Mexico border as part of a course he was taking on immigrants' rights at Vassar. Kathryn was funded for a GMAT review course; she is interested in pursuing an MBA degree to enhance her career in the corporate world.

The most recent grant went to my firstborn grandchild, Jessica, for an extraordinary, eight-week trip to South Africa. Jessica, a wild-animal trainer and manager, covered half the cost from her own savings and the Foundation underwrote the rest. Last March, when our family got together for Passover—and my 85th birthday celebration—Jessica narrated a fascinating slideshow of her journey. I was taken aback by the beauty of her photography of the creatures in the wild, of the African terrain and sunsets. Even more gratifying to me was the excitement in her voice and the delight in her eyes as she regaled us with tales of the animals she had observed for the first time in their natural habitats, of the interesting people she met and the unfamiliar culture she had embraced. It was hard to believe that this very confident, competent young woman had been identified with some learning disabilities as a young child. Through early intervention and hard work, she succeeded in overcoming those early deficits, in identifying her life's passion, and in forging her *very* unique path.

Jessica's slideshow elicited much enthusiasm and many interesting questions from the rest of the family. It was Teaching-and-Learning at its best. Through my granddaughter's trained eye, I was thrilled to see a part of the world that I will likely never visit and was thrilled to be part of the "village" that helped her to get there.

LIVING LEGACY FOUNDATION
REQUEST

A. SUBMITTED BY:_____DATE:_____

PREFERRED EMAIL:_____

PROPOSED PROJECT/ACTIVITY/PURCHASE (P/A/P)

B. P/A/P AND LINK TO ITS WEBSITE:

_____

_____

C. BRIEFLY: WHY DO YOU WANT TO UNDERTAKE THIS P/A/P? HOW DO YOU BELIEVE YOU (AND/OR OTHERS) WILL BENEFIT?_____

_____

_____

D. WHAT IS THE TIMEFRAME OF THE P/A/P, AND BY WHEN DO YOU NEED THE LIVING LEGACY FOUNDATION'S CONTRIBUTION?_____

_____

_____

BUDGET

E. AMOUNT REQUESTED FROM LLF: $

F. TOTAL BUDGET FOR P/A/P: $

IF THE LLF IS A PARTIAL FUNDER, HOW WILL YOU COVER THE REST?

_____

_____

_____

G. ITEMIZE KEY EXPENSES ASSOCIATED WITH THE P/A/P (IF APPLICABLE)

Item	*Amount*	*Funded by*
	$	
	$	
	$	
	$	
	$	
TOTAL COST:		

FOLLOW-UP

H. WHAT SORT OF "TEACHING-AND-LEARNING" EXPERIENCE WILL YOU BE PROVIDING THE FAMILY? (*Example: share travel journal or photos, report on a course or conference; explain how equipment/product/activity helps your work or enriches your life, brings you closer to your goals, helps you identify your passions.*)_____

_____

I. ADDITIONAL COMMENTS:

BOARD DECISION

1. LIVING LEGACY FOUNDATION'S CONTRIBUTION:
$_____

2. HOW/WHEN WILL THE MONEY BE TRANSMITTED?_____
_____
_____

3. IF THE REQUEST WAS DENIED, OR IF DOLLAR AMOUNT WAS LESS (OR MORE) THAN REQUESTED, THE REASON WAS:_____
_____
_____

4. BOARD MEMBERS' COMMENTS/SUGGESTIONS, IF ANY: (*can be email thread*)_____
_____
_____
_____
_____

"ALWAYS LEAVE YOUR CAMPSITE BETTER THAN YOU FOUND IT."
— JERRY WITKOVSKY

"Three Jars": A Living Legacy for Younger Children

Recently, another grandchild was welcomed as a new member of the board, with full voting rights. My son created a lovely certificate to present to his newly Bat Mitzvah'ed daughter, Merete, in commemoration of this expanded role.

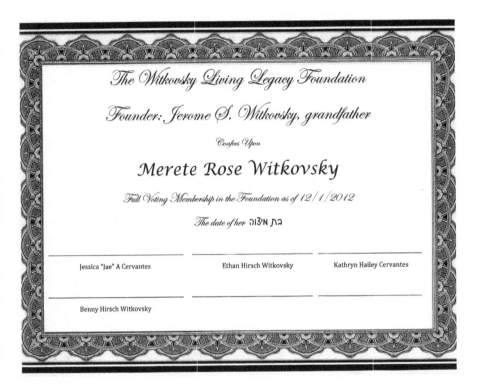

The Witkovsky Living Legacy Foundation

Founder: Jerome S. Witkovsky, grandfather

Confers Upon

Merete Rose Witkovsky

Full Voting Membership in the Foundation as of 12/1/2012

The date of her בת אי3וה

Jessica "Jae" A Cervantes   Ethan Hirsch Witkovsky   Kathryn Hailey Cervantes

Benny Hirsch Witkovsky

But even grade-schoolers are old enough to start learning to make smart choices about their money and to take pride in financial "independence." That's why—again, with my children's blessings—I instituted the program of "Three Jars." I purchased three mason jars, labeling one for "Saving," one for "Spending," and one for "Helping" (meaning, charitable giving). I put a modest amount of cash in each one and contribute a few dollars every month. Their allowances from their parents, their birthday or holiday gifts, their earnings from odd jobs (like lawn work or shoveling snow around the neighborhood)—all are apportioned within the three jars that stand side-by-side in the children's bedrooms. (The savings eventually make their way into their bank accounts or other investments, and they can study up on worthy charities they'd like to contribute to.)

The "Three Jars"—a concept I don't claim to have originated, by the way—gives younger grandchildren a strong visual representation of where their money is going and what it can do; it helps them to experience firsthand the discipline of saving, the importance of giving, and the pleasure of buying. During a recent family outing, I was tickled to see Merete buy herself a carefully chosen souvenir of a delicate ring, taking obvious pride in the fact that she had paid for it out of her "Spending" jar. Similarly, each week, she is expected to bring a dollar to Hebrew school, to contribute to charity; instead of asking her parents for the cash, she always makes sure she has it in hand, taking it from her "Helping" jar before she gets into the car.

In the words of the Chinese philosopher Lao Tzu: **"Give a man a fish and you feed him for a day. Teach a man to fish and you feed him for a lifetime."** My hope is that the education of the Three Jars will inculcate habits and ideals that will carry on long after my grandchildren have moved on from those childhood bedrooms.

Keep an Eye on the "Valuables"

In evaluating our legacy, it is also crucial to take a cold, hard look at the "valuables" part of the equation. The reality is, even when everyone has the best of intentions, clashes over money have traditionally ranked high among the most common and serious stressors of family life. And current demographic and economic trends could exacerbate this. The MetLife Mature Market Institute points out that the average age for becoming a first-time grandparent today (according to the latest U.S. Census) is 50 for women and 54 for men. Far from fitting the stereotype of those dependent "ancients" of yore, most boomer grandparents are still working, and many are in better financial shape than their adult offspring: "Incomes of households headed by those ages 55 or older rose by $491 from 2000 to 2009, while those in the 25-34 and 35-44 age groups saw their incomes decline; 45- to 54-year-olds had just a $42 increase." *(https://www.metlife.com/about/press-room/us-press-releases/2011/index.html? compID=50460)*

The MetLife study indicates that grandparents' spending reflects this relative prosperity to the tune of $2.43 billion annually on grandkids' primary and secondary school tuitions alone (approximately 2.5 times greater than the $853 million they spent in 1999). Says Sandra Timmermann, director of the Institute:

> *The increased financial instability of today's younger families, has huge business implications. The fact that grandparents are spending a great deal of money on infant food and equipment, children's clothing, toys, elementary and secondary school tuition, and financial, mortgage and insurance products, represents a change in buying habits and may change the way marketers and advertisers focus their efforts.*

So what's a responsible grandparent to do? First and foremost, make sure your financial house is in order. There are countless books and online resources to guide you, but **I strongly recommend that you engage a licensed financial professional (unless you yourself are one) to figure out what works best in your circumstances.**

Here are a few very basic "dos and don'ts" to consider.

- DO set a good example by being communicative and candid about financial matters, paving the way for your adult children to do the same. You needn't eschew privacy altogether, but there shouldn't be taboos about discussing important money matters within the family. (Reading and discussing articles about money, for example, is an excellent agenda for Family Meetings.)

- DO make sure that the language in your final directives and in your will is explicit and clear. Vague instructions or "surprises" can set the stage for conflict. Because the laws do change, and frequently vary from state to state in regard to estates, taxation, and health care, an attorney who specializes in **eldercare** is considered the most reliable last word in these matters.

- DON'T put others' needs before your own financial security. It is tempting to want to lavish gifts upon grandchildren or to help them (or their parents) out of tight spots. But it is important to make a careful assessment of your own long-term needs first before giving major gifts or even loans to family members. The last thing you want to do is to have to rely upon them later, because you've exhausted your resources.

- DON'T "enable" grandchildren by automatically underwriting big-ticket items. Allow them to develop the skills to achieve financial independence. It's bad news all around if their response to your generosity shifts from appreciation to expectation.

- DO educate yourself about giving wisely. For example, there are estate-planning benefits to making annual monetary gifts directly to grandchildren, if you are financially able to do so. At the same time, many people are unaware that a well-meaning contribution to a grandchild's college fund could end up hurting his or her chances of getting financial aid. Once again, it is important to check in with a financial advisor.

(http://www.grandparents.com/money-and-work/family-finance/6-common-money-mistakes-grandparents-make (Oct. 7, 2012); http://www.dailyfinance.com/2013/03/07/college-financial-aid-529-plan-mistakes-grandparents/)

My Legacy

What do I dream of when I contemplate *my* legacy? I dream that the activities that the Witkovsky Living Legacy Foundation underwrites will continue to enrich the lives of my family members and the lives of others. I dream that, in the future, my grandchildren will have the means and the motivation to fund the Foundation themselves; I dream that they will build in a philanthropic component and actively support causes that they agree are important to all of them. And I dream that they will pass along the Foundation as a treasured family tradition to their grandchildren someday.

Well, I can't see that far into the future; and besides—as my son often reminds me—it's important to savor the present. And I do. I savor the laughter and connection of my grandchildren, those far-flung siblings and cousins, as I watch them discover their individual passions and share their experiences and ideas with each other.

THE GRANDCHILDREN SPEAK

PLAYING THE MARKET WITH GAGGIE

Not every teenager has an octogenarian investment guru who he telephones daily and refers to as "Gaggie." But thanks to my grandmother Rita Butensky, I've fallen in love with playing the stock market like I used to play Fantasy Football.

It all started several years ago when Gaggie bought 10 shares of Disney for my two brothers and me. After seeing how profitable it was, I eagerly began purchasing some stocks on my own: Apple, Google, and Verizon. (Being a triplet, I often do things in threes.) Now, the minute I get home from school, I rush to my computer to see how my stocks are doing, and then I call Gaggie to discuss the market. She always has the same cautionary message: "Great job, Ari, but remember . . . I was lucky."

Gaggie started investing at a time when the economy was much more robust, hitting it big with AT&T before it split into the Baby Bells. She constantly exhorts me to buy a stock only after learning everything I can about the company, to follow all of my stocks closely, and to proceed cautiously in this volatile global market. She is adamant that it would be foolish for today's young investors to rely solely on luck.

Whenever the red arrow of doom appears on my screen, I break into a sweat over my decreasing portfolio. And then I call Gaggie. Her comforting words and common-sense wisdom remind me that you can't always win; and that in the stock market, just like in life, sometimes you just have to accept a loss and move on.

Through hard work and dedication, and with Gaggie's sound advice, I'm hoping that I too will be "lucky."

ARI SCHEINTHAL (19)
Cherry Hill, New Jersey

GRANDPA WALT'S GIFT OF HISTORY

My grandfather, Walter Roswell Truman Smith, is a collector of early American woodworking tools. I love visiting him and Grandma Daisy in Connecticut and exploring their eighteenth-century barn filled with thousands of tools from every imaginable trade.

Grandpa knows the history behind every single tool in his collection. A few years ago, the popular TV series "Antiques Roadshow" was coming to Washington, DC, near where I live; it's my mom's favorite show, so my dad got us tickets. I asked Grandpa whether he had anything that might be fun to get appraised. He gave me a woodworking plane stamped with the name "Cesar Chelor," the first documented African-American toolmaker in North America.

On the day of the show's taping I waited at the "tool table" until it was my turn with the appraiser. I showed him the plane and repeated everything that Grandpa had told me about Cesar Chelor: that he had originally been a slave belonging to this country's earliest known plane-maker, a man named Francis Nicholson; and shortly before Nicholson's death in 1753, he gave Chelor his freedom, and bequeathed Chelor his workshop and the tools to keep it going.

The appraiser was very quiet while he carefully examined the tool. I was really excited (and a little nervous) when he loudly announced: "This needs to go on the show!" The crew immediately began filming us.

Grandma and Grandpa thought it was so cool to see me on national television when the segment aired a few weeks later. Apparently my grandfather had given me an amazing gift, probably the "jewel" of his entire collection. It turned out to be worth over $6,000!

It would be just like my grandpa not to have made a big deal about it.

I feel very lucky to be related to this world-class tool collector/ home-builder/fire-builder/gardener/squirrel-catcher. I can't imagine any better company. (Except maybe Grandma: world-class macaroni-and-cheese-maker/carrot-cake-baker.)

JACK T. (13)
Virginia

ABSENCE IS PRESENCE

When I reflect on my grandparents, it seems mostly a story of absence, fused with curiosity and imagination and great respect.

All four of my grandparents died by the time I was five—both grandfathers well before my birth; Fanny had a heart attack (in her sleep) when I was three, and Lilly was taken by a painful, invasive cancer soon two years later.

The few fleeting images I retain are of Lilly rocking me on an antique rocking chair (Fanny's) in my bedroom. I clearly recall the rhythmic creaking of the wood as it etched the floor, and the feel of her arms around me, the softness and safety of her broad lap—as I melted into her.

Stories still circulate about Fanny's dedication to playing catch with me when I was two and three years old. She apparently escorted me regularly to our yard to nurture my athletic abilities—clearly helping train my incredibly accurate left throwing arm, which resulted in my ascent to team captain throughout my school years.

Lilly's youngest sister, Mollie, outlived Lilly by 25 years, and with her I shared wonderful moments in her Fairfax district apartment, lounging on her overstuffed sofa while she rubbed my back and regaled me with stories of her Eastern Star excursions to Hawaii and beyond. I was always aware of the scent of powder when I entered Mollie's house; it was a comforting and evocative fragrance at the time, and sometimes it felt as if we daydreamed in tandem during those slow-motion, gentle afternoons. She lived not far from the La Brea Tar Pits, and my mother often drove us to the back entrance of the art museum so that we could stroll the grounds, rest on benches beside the sluggish pools of oil, ponder the enormous wooly mammoths whose legs had become trapped in the thick deposits, and end our visit amidst the boisterous crowds at Cantor's Deli.

Still, I wished I had been able to share such experiences with my grandparents, but I was born late, to older parents. Even though decades have passed, I occasionally find myself wondering: what might their laughter have sounded like? What ideas dominated their thoughts? What were their tastes in art, music, poetry? What life-lessons would they have conveyed to me, the youngest of all the grandchildren?

And what of their global perspective? Though only once-removed from the *shtetl* experience, would they have embraced learning about different cultures and wished to travel the world to absorb and observe more? Were any of them adventurers at heart? Or scholars? (Or would they have been packing-averse and largely cowardly about travel, like my parents?)

What would they say if they had seen me teaching and joking with university students in India, Africa, Eastern Europe, and more? And what of their faith, and their degree of practice and belief? Might they be scarred by the xenophobia and insularity that plague so many? Would they be joyful in welcoming their soon-to-be-born great-great-grandchild, who will enter this world half-Japanese and half-American, a fusion of Jewish, Buddhist, and Shintoist traditions?

It is clear that they each helped shape me, just as one's DNA inheritance and early synapse-formations set the stage for our future growth, verbal abilities, associative powers, capacity for abstraction, and poetic sensibilities. Indeed, their imprint exists on the very cognitive and imaginative processes that I take for granted, the reflexive ones that allow me to craft this small essay. I reflect upon the wealth of gifts they bequeath to me, with gratitude. Though mine is largely a story of evanescent elders, their legacy endures, partly in the questions that have lingered.

G. S. EISEN (52)
Santa Barbara, California

Journaling Expedition #8:

Your "Ethical Will"

The tradition of creating an ethical will harkens back to Biblical times and is enjoying resurgence these days, according to Rabbi Jack Riemer, who made an exhaustive study of the practice for his book, *Ethical Wills: A Modern Treasury* (ed. *Jack Riemer and Nathaniel Stampfer, Schocken Books*).

Rabbi Riemer's book is one of many resources in libraries, bookstores, and online that can guide you in the preparation of an ethical will. Some of these materials are faith-based; others are not. Some have elaborate templates, while others are free-flowing, more informal, or shorter. There are primers on how to create video or audio ethical wills as well.

If having an ethical will appeals to you, use this journaling section to put down some thoughts about what to include, in whatever fashion is the most comfortable and natural for you. For inspiration, here are some ideas from Dr. Riemer's book that you can use as jumping-off points, courtesy of www.ourlifecelebrations.com, a blog hosted by Hospice Care of the West:

- Formative life events and experiences
- The era and world from which I came
- Important life lessons
- Influential people that shaped my life
- Some of my favorite possessions and the stories they contain
- Scriptural passages that guided and inspired me
- The mistakes I've made that I hope you don't repeat
- A true definition of success
- How I feel as I look back over my life
- I ask your forgiveness for . . .
- How grateful I am to you for . . .
- And finally, I want you to know I love you.

*Add your own prompts, if you wish:*_____

_____

_____

_____

_____

Thoughts about my ethical will:_____

_____

_____

_____

_____

_____

CHAPTER IX

THE GRANDCHILDREN SPEAK (WITKOVSKY EDITION)

"Grandchildren are the lines that connect the dots from generation to generation."

—Lois Wyse

L-R: Benny Witkovsky, Kathryn Cervantes, Aidan Witkovsky (in front of Grandpa), Ethan Witkovsky, Erin Beser (Ethan's wife), Merete Witkovsky, Jessica Cervantes (2013).

I know what I *tried* to Teach my grandchildren through the years, but what did they Learn? Several years ago, I asked them to write me a letter and tell me. They told me, all right!

AIDAN WITKOVSKY

Dear Grandpa;

1. You taught me to:
2. speak up it is fun to play with all ages
3. play chess
4. you supported me when I learning to ride a bike

I can't think of the other things you have taught me. But, I remember how much fun you teaching me is!

Sincerely, **AIDAN** (10)

MERETE WITKOVSKY

Dear Grandpa;

Over the course of my life, you have taught me many things. You've taught me to sweep kitchen floors, to speak louder, to play chess, to help cook, to help set the table, and how to manage my money. You've helped me manage my money by giving me three jars for my bat mitzvah, labeled "Save," "Spend," and "Charity" *(tzedakah)* and giving me $15 each month to sort into them.

These jars that you gave me have given me a lot to think about. Each month I have to decide where to put the money, with a general idea that it wouldn't be the greatest thing to put all $15 in the Saving or Spending jars (as much as I would've liked to). So I do the math to separate it equally, leaving $5 for each jar.

I haven't used a single dollar from my Savings jar. I've given quite a lot of my Tzedakah money during Sunday or Hebrew School, or just donating if I have money with me when we go out to shelters, etc. Sure, I'll admit I have used a lot of the spending money, but it's for spending, so I'm allowed too. With the money I have spent, I've spent it on things that

I need, or if I go to the store and I forget to bring money with me and I want to get something, my mom buys it and I pay her back.

That's what I've learned and that's how I use my money jars. Thank you!

Your Granddaughter, **MERETE** (13)

BENNY WITKOVSKY

Dear Grandpa,

I am confused—but then again, so are you. I'm not sure if this letter is supposed to be about specific things—ideas, skills, bits of wisdom—that I have learned from you. Or if it is supposed to be about the way I watch you interact with the world and how I see those same traits in myself. And I don't think you know what you want the letter to be about either.

I think that your goal is for these letters to help build the family as a "Teaching-And-Learning community." If you want the family to be a vessel for learning skills and ideas, then why does it matter what specifically I learned from you? Isn't the process the important thing to cultivate and propose to others? The Family Meeting in which ideas are shared and discussed, the family book club, or just the planned lessons in a certain thing. But I don't really remember any one idea from a Family Meeting, I never read any of the books, and I would have learned to ride a bike or to play tennis on my own. The family does not act as the perfect vessel for education; the education acts as your tool through which to build a family. So again, why does it matter what I learned from you? Isn't it only the fact that I did learn from you? And the understanding of that process and creating it comes not from my letter, but from yours.

That's why I think what really interests you is the way of being that you have passed on. But then why is that something that should be written and published? I have told you before, so I think you know. And how does it serve as a teaching tool? You cannot change or craft your way of being to teach me. As I believe I have told you, "you don't get to chose what I watch and learn from you, it happens no matter what." So the family is a tool for teaching personality, intentionally and unintentionally, without a letter or a meeting or a plan.

Then I realize that I said this to you some five or six years ago. You have been playing with the same basic idea for ten years. You have changed the names, processes, theories, modes of presentation, but basically you have always been concerned with how the grandparent ensures that their essence is passed on either through a living legacy, teachable moments, or a family learning community.

It is that commitment to an idea that I have learned from you. I have watched you redefine your quest as you have been turned down, encouraged, and questioned. I have seen you take some criticism and ignore others. And I have learned how to explore an idea that you know has some inherent truth but that you are ceaselessly morphing and searching for the best way to define, understand and present. I don't know what my idea will be yet, but I hope I own it with the same conviction.

Love, **BENNY** (written at 17)

KATHRYN (KATIE) CERVANTES

I remember it like it was yesterday—the times I spent in downtown Chicago in my grandparents' old apartment. I remember family dinners, I remember playing dominos in the living room, I remember my grandparents cooking. I remember "swimming" in my grandmother's "messy room." However of all the memories, what I remember the most is playing catch with my grandpa in his back room. It felt like hours were spent back there with a package of tennis balls, and my grandpa repeating one line over and over (and over): "Katie, always keep your eye on the ball!"

I enjoyed playing catch and as I grew older I played softball, soccer and basketball—and through the years my grandpa would continue telling me to keep my eye on the ball. No matter what sport it is you have to be determined and stay focused.

Well, I soon learned that keeping your eye on the ball did not only have to be about a tennis or soccer ball, but was a way of thinking about life and keeping focused on anything you wanted. If you want something enough, you need to work hard and keep track of the objective no matter what it is.

I know that what I've learned from my grandparents will help me through the rest of my life. I've come to believe that grandparents are truly teachers to their grandchildren—that it is not only the parents' responsibility—because of the luck of knowing because the loving and amazing grandparents I have been blessed with.

Overall I could not be more grateful to have a family that is open with feelings and communicates well with each other. I also feel fortunate to have grown up in a well-rounded environment that has always involved "playing" together on vacations and participating in outdoor activities, as well as observing religious holidays and serious family discussions . . . all built upon the foundation created by my grandparents.

As great as all the memories are, when asked to put in writing what I have learned from my grandparents, I wanted to be sure to do it justice by expressing the impact of their unconditional love. This love they have given me and the rest of our family a foundation to live a happy, healthy life . . . no matter what our road or how curvy it may be, along the way. What I carry with me the most from my grandparents is fairly simple: to be a good person and a good family member, and to play an active role in every community I am a part of.

Love, **KATHRYN** (written at 25)

ETHAN WITKOVSKY

Dear Grandpa,

You have asked me to tell you what I have learned from you. This exercise is an example of the single most important lesson I have learned from you, Grandpa: show your family that you care about who they are and always keep them talking. You constantly ask me how I am, what I am doing, why I am doing things, etc., and you really want to know the answer. You have made me share my school papers with you from ninth grade through my third year of grad school. I think that this single action is one of the most caring things anyone has done for me. For any groups that my grandfather is sharing this with, I will emphasize this point: always ask to read people's papers; always show that you care about your family—not just because they are your family, but because you are interested in who they are.

Another thing that this reminds me of is that I have learned from you is to never be afraid to look weird or silly. I mean really, Grandpa . . . asking your grandchildren (and probably tons of other random folks in your life) to write letters to their grandparents? Most people would think that was weird. Actually most people (well, the people I have asked to write letters at least) start out by saying "that's kind of weird," then they think about it for a minute and decide that it is actually really sweet. You have taught me to never be afraid to look foolish doing something I think is worthwhile. You have shown me to go after what I want without timidity. "You think you want to be a rabbi? Go sit down with a rabbi and talk to him then follow him around for a week." "Oh, you are interested in summer camps? Go sit down with a camp director and meet with them, then follow them around for a week." "*You want to be a spy?*" . . . etc. Grandpa, you have taught me to seek the knowledge I need and to speak to the right people.

You have also not merely supported what I thought I wanted; you added your own two cents as well. "You want to be a rabbi? First go work in a factory and meet real people." "You are interested in summer camps? Don't work at a summer camp! Go work in a factory and meet real people." (Said the man who spent approximately 30 years working in a summer camp and approximately zero years working in a factory.) These suggestions are all part of your caring for me. The lesson to go and make sure I know what life is like for all different kinds of people has been an important one to me. (And I apologize for never having worked in a factory.)

And, of course, Grandpa, no letter about what you have taught me could be finished without your famous phrase that I will never forget and that I will continue to use in every application and personal statement I write: "Always leave your campsite better than you found it." Right after teaching me to love and be interested in my family, you taught me to love and care for the world around me. I have learned from your words and from your actions that the world should be better, not worse, for having housed me. I live my life to try and make all the campsites I use, better; you have shown me not only that I need to make them better, but you have also given me glimpses of how to do so.

I am sure that I will add to this letter or want to change it (you have also taught me never to stop revising things I have written) but this is what I have for now. I love you and I will call you soon.

Thank you for reading my papers,
ETHAN (written at 26)

Dear Grandma Margaret,

I know that this might seem a little weird, writing you a letter even though you left us many years ago, but your husband asked me to write you a letter and I pretty much won't say no to Grandpa. I am going to resist the urge to ask about how you are doing and what you are up to but I will tell you that I am well. I am in rabbinical school now and I am working on ways of bringing an old religion to people through new technologies (and also some old technologies too). My dad told me once that you predicted when I was born that this is what I would do with my life. Nice job! Actually I think that I learned a lot about faith from you. The predictions and star-chart stuff, not to mention tarot cards and previous lives, were perhaps all about your belief in the unseen and that there are forces at work in our universe that are beyond our mien but that we can tap into briefly and rudimentarily if we go about it in the right way.

In fact, Grandma, as I write this I realize that I completely share in your belief in the power and magic of the world around us and that I would not be who I am today without it, or without you. You taught me that it is okay to have faith, and that belief and love of these things is not silly and doesn't make you silly. On that same note you also taught me to enjoy little things other people miss, and that there is cool stuff to be found in even mundane things like puzzles and wearing purple. You taught me that nothing should be overlooked and that if you note and remember everything you see, you will be really, really good at crossword puzzles.

You taught me that messy rooms can be a lot of fun and I inherited, or learned, that same trait from you. It is a trait that says you want to be able to do anything and everything (because anything and everything can be cool) and don't have time to pick up things, or need to have them in neat piles or put away. If there is a path to walk through and I know where everything in the room is, why should I clean it up more than that? However you also showed me the dangers of such a life and such a room. The pitfalls of half-finished quilts and paintings, the lost items that infuriate ("I know it is in the room *somewhere*") and the need for maybe a little bit of order. You taught me mostly through example that there is a dangerous quality to the mixture of passion, intellect and scattered enthusiasm for everything that runs in our family. I both relish and fear the fact that I exhibit many of the qualities that you did in this regard.

This is where I would like to finish my letter to you, Grandma. You taught me many little things about puzzles, marble runs, games, food, painting, poker and not to fight with my cousins. Really, though, it was the big things that will stay with me and are the most influential in my life. Your sense of play, the passion for life, the discipline and the faith in a magical universe have all been transmitted to me through a combination of teaching and DNA. These things have been a part of making me who I am today, for better and for worse, and they will continue to guide me as I go forward. Thank you, Grandma, for all of the things you gave me, and for being a ready teacher and playmate.

I miss you and love you,
ETHAN (written at 26)

ERIN BESER

Dear Grandpa,

First of all—thanks for letting me call you Grandpa. My maternal grandfather died before I was born and my paternal grandfather died when I was eight, so it's been a long time since I've had a Grandpa in my life. Grandparents are important characters in the narrative of a human being, playing the critical role of keepers of memory and custodians of legacy.

You've only been my grandfather-in-law for a little over a year, but in my years of getting to know you following my engagement and marriage to Ethan, I've learned a lot from you. I've learned how to welcome newcomers into a family and how to create a culture of learning from one another that is ever evolving and expanding. You have made living a legacy your lasting gift to your family and I am so honored and proud to now be included in this lucky group of people.

Thank you, Grandpa.
ERIN (28)

JESSICA ANNE CERVANTES

When you're part of a family, you learn from each other. Parents teach their children, and children teach their parents. Sometimes children are lucky enough to have grandparents in their lives. I happened to be exceptionally lucky and grew up with a wonderful grandfather and grandmother. My mother's parents have played a very large role in my life. I am sure I cannot recall all of the things that my grandparents have taught me, but here are a few highlights.

When I was a little girl, my grandfather—a frequent tennis player— would keep a lot of tennis balls around. There was always one of those tall cans around, filled with fuzzy yellow balls. He would always play catch with me, and his mantra was "keep your eye on the ball." When playing catch, and in life in general, he taught me that if you focus on your target or goal you will be more likely to reach it. (Plus, it probably improved my hand-eye coordination.) Later, as I was growing up, Grandpa would come and watch me take tennis lessons. It wasn't really my thing, but he was always there supporting me.

In addition to being the general director of a major community center system, Grandpa was the director of an overnight camp, Camp CHI (Chicago Hebrew Institute). Camp has always been a very special place for my family; it was my home away from home, growing up. I first visited Camp CHI when I was just three months old and continued going there for summers and other occasions with my family throughout my teens. So many lessons were taught to me at camp, some from my grandparents, and some observed on my own. I truly believe that my love for nature and wildlife began at camp. (Located just outside of the Wisconsin Dells, Camp CHI is tucked away in the woods on Lake Delton.)

One special thing that my grandfather and I would do together at camp was waking up before sunrise to watch the deer. We would walk to the lake and quietly observe the deer drinking from the lake as the sun rose. It was always a spectacular sight. I learned that sometimes you can take enormous pleasure in the most basic aspects of nature and life. Never being a morning person, I learned that getting up early can be very rewarding, and that to witness nature in its full form you have to be very quiet and patient. Going to camp during the summertime, I furthered my passion by horseback riding and spending time at the petting zoo. I also developed a love for rock-climbing on the rock wall. Grandpa also let me do my first bit of driving at camp when I was just a preteen. We used a golf cart on the dirt trails; it was a lot of fun.

My favorite lesson that I learned from my grandfather at camp is to "always leave your campsite BETTER than you found it." If you are camping and you see trash on the ground, pick it up and throw it out. Even if it's not yours it's not a difficult thing to do and it makes a huge difference restoring the natural beauty of the land.

Camp CHI is a Jewish camp, so it is also about community. My grandfather has always been very connected to the Jewish community. For him, religion is a lot more than belief in G-d or historical events. It is about bringing people together and forming bonds as a group. It's about learning together, growing together, sharing personal experiences, and supporting each other. Having a personal connection with Judaism means that you are always part of a community—that you can move somewhere where you do not know anyone and make friends with people through going to temple or taking classes.

My grandmother taught me a lot about art, performance, and mystical possibilities. Grandma loved to draw, sew, and perform—she was very theatrical. She would help my cousins, sister, and me perform plays during family vacations. She was also open to the possibilities of past-life experiences and other forms of astrology. She also showed me that you never stop learning. In an age where technology is constantly changing, my grandmother was able to keep up with new computer technologies—she even taught other senior citizens how to use them. She also sometimes struggled with depression; however, she never really let it greatly affect her relationships with her family. She was always able to have fun with us grandchildren, and was even goofy sometimes.

When I was little, Grandpa taught me how to count using the change in his small ceramic desk bank. We would dump out all of the money, separate it and count it. He helped motivate me by allowing me to keep some of the money. When I got older, it was important to him to teach me that I had to share the money with my sister. My grandfather has always been very modest with his money. He has never felt the need to drive a luxury vehicle or go on fancy vacations around the world. Instead, he would rather be able to always help out a family member in need, financially. He has helped out most of his grandchildren with college finances. He has helped me personally with rent while attending college. He has helped out my parents and other family members when they've had economic troubles. For him, family is always more important than how much money is in the bank. The generous fund he set up for our "Living Legacy Foundation" encourages siblings and cousins to stay in touch with each other and to help each other in achieving our dreams and goals.

Grandpa also has taught me that family means that you love each other unconditionally—that you cannot hold grudges, and are expected to forgive one another. He believes that to make mistakes in life is part of being human, and if you learn from your mistakes, then you can move forward. He talks out issues, and tells family members when he has felt hurt by them. Opening up a conversation about the issue teaches both parties and allows room for forgiveness.

Finally, some of the other very important lessons that my grandfather has taught me include:

"There is no such thing as a stupid question."

"You are never done learning."

"You can do anything that you put your mind to."

"You didn't fail if you tried your best."

"Follow your passions."

Love, **JESSICA** (written at 28)

Journaling Expedition #9:

Your Grandchildren Speak

1. If you asked your grandchildren (now or when they are old enough), *"what did I teach you?"* what do you think they would say?

_____

_____

_____

_____

_____

_____

2. Ask them! Have them write you a letter or an email, if they're willing, or just talk about it. What did they say? Were there any surprises, positive or negative?

_____

_____

_____

_____

_____

_____

_____

CHAPTER X

ALL-OF-A-KIND GRANDKIDS: RESOURCES FOR UNDERSTANDING AND HOPE

"Fixing is the illness mode. Acceptance is the identity mode."
—Andrew Solomon
(Far from the Tree: Parents, Children and the Search for Identity)

"The trouble with a close family is that it suffers closely, too."
—Roger Rosenblatt *(Making Toast: A Family Story)*

This book has emphasized the inestimable value of striving to be the most engaged grandparents we can imagine being. This is true even—or maybe *especially*—when life doesn't go exactly how we imagined.

A grandparent's steadfast love and support can be a godsend when families face bumps in the road or are blindsided by events that shake their very foundations. Like what happened to noted journalist Roger Rosenblatt and his wife, who were happily planning their retirement when the unthinkable happened: their daughter, Amy, a physician and the married mother of three small children, died suddenly of an undetected heart ailment. The Rosenblatts' own grief had to take a backseat to the immediate needs of the young family that was rocked by Amy's passing. With their son-in-law's blessing, "Boppo and Mimi" packed up their lives and moved in with him and the children—the story at the heart of Roger Rosenblatt's eloquent and moving memoir, *Making Toast*.

When one of the grandkids asked how long they were staying, Rosenblatt replied: "forever." Thus, they joined the ranks of the 4.5 million American grandparents (according to MetLife) who live under the same roof as their grandchildren. In the majority of cases, nowadays, this occurs out of economic necessity (mostly, the children's) brought about by unemployment, divorce, single parenthood, or illness.

Life's "unexpecteds" can come in many different forms. In an acclaimed new book based on interviews with more than 300 families, author Andrew Solomon examines the struggles and triumphs of children who are the proverbial "apples who've fallen" (in the words of its title) *Far from the Tree*. With immense sensitivity, Solomon applies this aphorism to youngsters with vastly differing stories—from those identified as having autism, transgender identities, Down syndrome, schizophrenia, and multiple disabilities, to those exhibiting criminal behavior or the genius of prodigies. Solomon's impetus for writing the book was his own painful journey to self-acceptance and family healing, having himself been "far from the tree." As a dyslexic child, he benefitted from his parents' strong advocacy—but was crushed by their lack of understanding and support when he later came out as gay.

Solomon's inspirational message is that while all families face challenges and are different in some ways, none of us need feel we are alone. From his book's website www.farfromthetree.com: **"While each of these characteristics is potentially isolating, the experience of difference within families is universal, as are the triumphs of love . . ."**

You may already be quite familiar with what it means to fall far from the tree. Perhaps one or more of your own children fit under that heading—or you yourself did, a very long time ago. Regardless, as grandparents, we are likely to be pained on two fronts: we worry for our beloved grandchild, wanting desperately for his or her road in life to be a smooth one; and our hearts go out to our adult offspring, who may be stressed beyond their limits. As the elders of the village that is helping to raise this child, we naturally want to do everything within our power to help.

What's the best way to do so? **Educate yourself.** It may be perfectly normal to feel sad or even devastated, depending on the situation. But don't panic, seek to blame, or heap on unasked-for advice. Take your cues from your adult children; be there to lend a helping hand or comforting shoulder whenever possible, but don't try and take over. Unless they beseech you that, for a time, for you to take over is exactly what they need.

As Andrew Solomon points out, isolation is one of the most devastating sequelae for families facing tough times. Thanks to the Internet, we've become a true global village, with access to state-of-the-art information, online support groups, and expert blogs. With this invaluable resource, however, come many minefields. Unregulated, unsubstantiated, and anecdotal information (that breeds unnecessary fears) is sometimes hard to differentiate from that which is authoritative, and even *reliable* information may not apply to your situation. When in doubt, contact an appropriate, licensed professional or support agency for accurate, up-to-date information regarding your specific circumstances.

The books, websites, and support organizations provided below are by no means comprehensive. They are the result of careful research, but this is not to say we endorse or take responsibility for any content.

Take heart, through the tough times. Take care of yourself. Rarely do our very worst fears come to pass. And even when they do come to pass we discover that are equal to them. And we grow as individuals and as families. As the saying goes:

"We may not have it all together . . . but together, we have it all."

A RESOURCE GUIDE FOR GRANDPARENTS

- **ABUSE**

http://aacap.org/page.ww?name=Child+Sexual+Abuse&section= Facts+for+Families—**Fact sheet on child sexual abuse from the** American Academy of Child and Adolescent Psychiatry.

http://www.domesticpeace.ca/documents/HelpingMy ChildGuide_000.pdf—Helping children when there is domestic violence in the home.

- **ADOPTION**

Gilman, Lois, *The Adoption Resource Book: Everything You Ought to Know About Creating an Adoptive Family*

www.adopthelp.com—Resources for adoptive families.

http://www.childwelfare.com/raising%20adopted%20children. htm—Bibliography of books on raising adopted children.

- **BEREAVEMENT/SERIOUS ILLNESS**

McCue, Kathleen and Bonn, Ron, *How to Help Children through a Parent's Serious Illness.*

www.childgrief.org—Resources for helping children prepare for the death of a loved one and dealing with the aftermath.

http://www.cancer.org/treatment/childrenandcancer/helpingchild renwhenafamilymemberhascancer/dealingwithaparentsterminal illness/dealing-with-a-parents-terminal-illiness-toc—Helping children to deal with a family member who is terminally ill.

http://www.cancercare.org/publications/50-helping_the_siblings _of_the_child_with_cancer—Helping siblings of seriously ill children, one of many fine resources from cancercare.org.

http://www.cancer.org/treatment/childrenandcancer/whenyour childhascancer/resources-for-parents-and-families-who-have-lost-a-child-to-cancer—For families coping with the death of a child.

http://childrenshospital.org/az/Site1705/Documents/parent_ guide2.pdf—Boston Children's Hospital's manual for helping children deal with hospitalizations and medical experiences.

http://www.rarediseases.org/—Comprehensive database of rare diseases, especially those affecting children.

http://www.ninds.nih.gov/—National Institutes of Health site on wide range of neurological diseases.

- **BIRTH DEFECTS**

http://www.marchofdimes.com—Clearing-house of information on heart defects, Down syndrome, spina bifida, cleft lip/palate, among others.

http://cerebralpalsy.org/

http://mda.org/—Muscular dystrophy

http://www.nlm.nih.gov/medlineplus/cysticfibrosis.html

- **BULLYING/CYBER BULLYING**

Thomas, Dr. Jason, Parent's Guide to Preventing and Responding to Bullying (from http://www.parenting.com/blogs/ mom-congress/melissa-taylor/best-5-bullying-books-parents)

http://www.stopbullying.gov/resources/index.html/—Resource center for dealing with bullying issues.

http://www.ncpc.org/topics/cyberbullying—Information and resources to stop cyber bullying from National Crime Prevention Council.

- **DIVORCE/GRANDPARENTS' RIGHTS**

Carson, Dr. Lillian, *The Essential Grandparents Guide to Divorce: Making a Difference in the Family*

http://www.grandparents.com/family-and-relationships/divorce/helpinggrandchildrenthroughparentdivorce—Guidance for grandchildren dealing with divorce.

http://www.ehow.com/about_5399243_grandparents-rights-divorce.html—Guide to grandparents' rights in divorce situations. *(Note: laws vary state by state. Consult a local grandparents' rights organization or family-law attorney.)*

- **CHILD HEALTH AND DEVELOPMENT**

http://health.nih.gov/category/ChildTeenHealth—National Institutes of Health site for childhood-specific health topics.

- **DRUGS AND ALCOHOL**

http://theparenttoolkit.org/images/uploads/toolkit/resource_files/grandparents_guide.pdf—How grandparents can help teenagers stay away from drugs and alcohol. One of many useful resources at http://www.drugfree.org/

http://theparenttoolkit.org/article/alcoholism-in-the-family-understanding-the-risk—How alcoholism in the family raises addiction risk in youngsters.

http://www.al-anon.alateen.org—Support for families of problem drinkers and substance abusers. *(Note: check the site for a meeting near you.)*

http://www.drivinglaws.org/topics/teen-driving-laws—About DUI arrests and other teen-driving issues.

- **GRANDPARENTS RAISING GRANDCHILDREN**

http://www.usa.gov/Topics/Grandparents.shtml—Government guide for grandparents raising grandchildren.

http://www.aarp.org/relationships/friends-family/info-08-2011/grandfamilies-guide-getting-started.html—One of many grandparenting resources from AARP.

http://www.childwelfare.gov/preventing/supporting/resources/grandparents.cfm—Supports and benefits for grandparents.

http://www.strengthforcaring.com/daily-care/caring-for-someone-with-developmental-disabilities/grandparents-raising-grandchildren-with-developmental-disabilities/—Resources for raising grandchildren with special needs.

- **HOMOSEXUALITY, GENDER-IDENTITY ISSUES**

http://www.aarp.org/relationships/family/info-03-2011/support_gay_children.html—AARP guide to supporting gay children and grandchildren.

http://www.minddisorders.com/Flu-Inv/Gender-identity-disorder.html—General guide to gender-identity disorders.

http://health.nytimes.com/health/guides/disease/gender-identity-disorder/overview.html—*New York Times'* guide to gender-identity issues.

http://www.pflagsacramento.org/journal—Dr. Ruth Westheimer, for the parents' support group PFLAG, which has branches in many American cities and towns.

http://www.glsen.org/cgi-bin/iowa/all/antibullying/index.html—Antibullying resources for LGBT children.

• LEARNING DIFFERENCES/SPECIAL NEEDS

Kirzner, Judy. *Help! My Grandchild Has ADHD: What These Children and Their Parents Wish You Knew.*

http://www.sciencedaily.com/releases/2010/04/100406125712.htm—Grandparents' role in helping children with autism.

http://www.aspergersyndrome.org/Articles/Especially-for-Grandparents-of-Children-With-Asper.aspx—Helping grandparents gain an understanding of Asperberger's syndrome.

http://www.smartkidswithld.org/—Support organization with information for families and children with learning disabilities.

• MENTAL HEALTH

http://www.mayoclinic.com/health/teen-eating-disorders/my01156—Guide to understanding eating disorders among tweens and adolescents. *(NOTE: the Mayo Clinic's comprehensive website offers authoritative information on a full range of physical and emotional ailments.)*

http://www.nationaleatingdisorders.org/—Resource center for issues related to eating disorders.

http://www.parents.com/health/mental/dealing-with-anxiety-in-children/—Help in dealing with children who suffer from anxiety.

http://www.mayoclinic.com/health/self-injury/DS00775—Guide to help family members identify signs of cutting and other forms of self-injury.

http://www.aacap.org/cs/root/facts_for_families/facts_for_ families_keyword_alphabetical—Type in key word (i.e., depression) to learn more from the American Academy of Child and Adolescent Psychiatry.

http://www.nimh.nih.gov/health/publications/suicide-a-major- preventable-mental-health-problem-fact-sheet/suicide-a-major- preventable-mental-health-problem.shtml—Suicide prevention.

http://www.apa.org/helpcenter/choose-therapist.aspx—Tips on how to choose a therapist.

http://www.psychiatry.org/mental-health—American Psychiatric Association page with links to keyword search.

http://www.nasponline.org/families/index.aspx—Many good tips from the National Association of School Psychologists on helping kids deal with school anxiety, school issues, fears of violence.

http://www.nctsn.org/—The National Child Traumatic Stress Network. Helping children to cope with terrorism, natural disasters, war, and other forms of trauma, including abuse and neglect.

- **SENIOR HEALTH/AGING**

http://health.nih.gov/category/SeniorsHealth—National Institute of Health site on health issues for seniors, including how to explain aging issues to others in the family.

http://www.healthinaging.org/—On seniors staying healthy, from the American Geriatrics Society.

http://www.alz.org/living_with_alzheimers_just_for_kids_and_ teens.asp—Helping children understand Alzheimer's disease.

- **STEP-GRANDPARENTING**

http://www.grandparents.com/family-and-relationships/family-matters/youre-a-stepgrandparent — The joys and challenges of becoming a step-grandparent.

http://edis.ifas.ufl.edu/fy038 — Realities of stepfamilies.

http://www.stepfamilies.info/articles/the-special-tie-grandparents.php — A site for building healthy stepfamilies.

Some of Jerry's Favorites *(which have also served as resources for this book):*

Maimonides by Sherwin B. Nuland, MD
Childhood and Society by Erik H. Erikson, Second Edition
The Magic of Children by Dr. Mark Freed and Dr. Robert D. Safian
The Price of Privilege by Madeline Levine, Ph.D.
Staring at the Sun by Irvin D. Yalom
Families and Family Therapy by Salvador Minuchin, MD
The Grandparent Solution by Arthur Kornhaber, MD
Contemporary Grandparenting by Arthur Kornhaber, MD
The New Face of Grandparenting by Don Schmitz
Successful Grandparenting by Claire Rayner
The New American Grandparent by Andrew J. Cherlin and Frank F. Furstenberg, Jr.
The Blessing of a Skinned Knee by Wendy Model, Ph.D.

THE GRANDCHILDREN SPEAK

A LIFE-CHANGING GIFT

My "Bubby" Marvis gave me a life-changing gift: unconditional love, acceptance, and respect at a time when I needed it the most.

Ten years ago, in my early twenties, I came out to her as a lesbian. Having grown up in a tight-knit, Orthodox-Jewish family and community, I was still struggling with own acceptance of my sexual orientation, and grappling with feelings of guilt and shame. But from the moment I came out to Bubby, she encouraged me to be open with her, asking me lots of questions and showing a keen interest in my life and well-being. When I introduced her to Gali, my girlfriend, Bubby welcomed her with open arms as well. Over the years, Bubby was always careful to include Gali in family gatherings, referring to the two of us affectionately as "my girls." Her warmth and support helped quell my fears of rejection and gave me the courage to come out to others who I suspected might be less accepting.

In 2011, surrounded by our friends and family, Gali and I were married in a joyful ceremony that I couldn't even have dreamt of, all those years ago. We stood underneath a wedding canopy made of a woven shawl that had belonged to my great-great-grandmother, a shawl that Bubby had given me at my bat mitzvah. My one sadness on that otherwise perfect day was that Bubby, who died in 2007, was not there to celebrate with us. But as I stood under that canopy, uniting with my soulmate, I fully felt Bubby's spirit—positive, open, embracing, and sharing in our happiness.

KEREN R. (32)
Brooklyn, New York

I MISS YOU

Dear Nana:

I drove by your old apartment on Pine Street with Jacob recently. It's still hard to believe that you lived over sixty years and raised two children in that tiny little space with Pop. You would have adored Jacob and I'm sorry the two of you never met. He'd have loved our weekly dinner dates. I still remember those creaky narrow stairs leading up to your apartment and how the smell of homemade pizza and lentil soup would waft down to greet me on Friday nights.

When I was little you indulged me with our tea parties for two and sleepovers. Remember how you'd give me a shiny stack of nickels and let me stay up late to play cards with you and your girlfriends? Then we'd wake up early and I'd grab that tattered box filled with Mom's old wedding photos from the bottom drawer of your dresser. I never got sick of looking at them and hearing your stories—it's a wonder I didn't wear out those album-pages.

As an adult I learned about strength and dignity from you. How hard it must have been for you to lose a daughter. I was so wrapped up in my own grief—I'm sorry if I wasn't there for you. You never lost your spirit and you showed me how to be a kinder, better person.

I'd be a lucky woman to have just a bit of you in me. I miss you. Love, Christy

CHRISTY GIBNEY
New York, New York

TEACHING ME HOW TO HELP OTHERS

During my senior year in high school, a friend of mine was battling serious depression, and cutting herself. Not knowing what to do, I reached out to my grandfather, a psychologist. He explained to me how depressed individuals who hurt themselves in this manner, actually do so to feel alive—to at least feel something. His knowledge and support helped me deal with this friend, and later on with a college friend on the verge of suicide. I wish I had a happier story of how my grandfather has impacted my life, but the real lesson I learned from him was how important it is to do right by those who are struggling with serious issues in their lives. If these are issues that you are not qualified to deal with, you need to identify the right person to help them.

ALEX COHEN (26)
Westport, Connecticut

WHAT HAPPENED TO A GRACEFUL DEATH?

My grandmother hasn't spoken my name in nearly ten years. More recently, I ceased to be her grandson. Sometimes I'm her son-in-law, sometimes I'm a cousin. She's told me that her father, who emigrated from Minsk more than a hundred years ago, used to talk about me all the time. My grandma is my grandma, and she will always be. We used to call her "Grandma Kugel" after her signature dish, but when she started to leave the oven on, we had to move her to an assisted living facility.

It's hard for a child to see someone on life support. It's absolutely terrifying, the tubes and the loud machines. The delight of "we're going to Grandma's house" has become, "we have to go visit Grandma."

My grandmother is nearly 100 years old. She's in hospice now. If she has another life-threatening incident, she will die. The last time I visited her was after her most recent stroke. When she saw me, her eyes bulged and she silently tilted her head to the side. I don't know if she knows who I am, but I do know that the sight of me is one of the few comforts she has left in this world. I wish I could be there every day, but that isn't realistic. Maybe someday it'll be easier for me to remember her kugel, but now I can only think of bedridden pain, a foggy mind, lost memories. With all the wonders of medical technology, I think our society has forgotten the value of a graceful death.

SPENCER R. BRONSON (22)
Los Angeles, California

ACTIVISM, INSPIRED BY A GRANDMOTHER

About a dozen years ago—when I was a middle-school student, like those I currently teach—my grandmother began sharing with me the details of her own teenage years. During the Holocaust, she was one of nearly 30,000 "Partisans"—Jewish and Russian fighters who resisted the Nazis, banding together in the Polish forests. As Grandma Sonia opened up, so did my whole world. I can hardly say that she had a "normal" youth, but that's what it was until 1939, when the Soviets occupied her Polish village, Luboml. In 1941, the Germans invaded and established a highly restrictive ghetto for the Jews, and the true nightmare began.

Sonia escaped into the surrounding forest with her parents and uncle in 1942. After enduring a horrendous winter on their own as fugitives, they managed to join with the Soviet Partisans. It was then that Sonia assumed the responsibilities of caring for wounded soldiers, guarding the camp at night, and using hand-grenades on missions to sabotage Nazi trains.

Despite our lives having been so different on the surface, I know that Sonia felt many of the same things I have felt, as a young woman going out into the world: growing out of girlhood shyness, leaving a protected family cocoon, experiencing the first stirrings of romance. Today, I find myself struggling to understand her frame of mind at two distinct life-junctures: that of the courageous teenager who fought for survival, and that of the 87-year-old woman who has come so far and is surrounded by people who love and admire her—yet who at times feels utterly alone and empty, as one of so few survivors.

Grandma bravely wrote and published a memoir several years ago, titled *Here, There Are No Sarahs*. There's a story in it I've known since childhood, and it always stuck with me. During the first, bitter-cold winter that her family hid in the Polish forest, they were extremely depressed—huddled together for warmth and hardly speaking, knowing they were hunted and their lives were in danger. A Ukrainian peasant named Tichon came upon them. He could have abandoned them or even turned them over to the Nazis. Instead, when he saw 16-year-old Sonia, he started to cry. "You older people have lived already," he wept, "but this child hasn't had the chance to live yet." Tichon became instrumental in the survival of Sonia and her family, bringing them desperately needed food, information, and hope. My grandmother's grateful recounting of this humble man's heroic acts taught me that each of us has the power to stand up against evil and injustice, by helping those in need.

As I've grown into adulthood, the more I have learned about Sonia's unexpected role as a resistance fighter, the more I feel the mandate to carry on her spirit. Clearly, she was fighting for her life, and I fight for justice and human rights because I have the luxury to do so. Still, I believe that we are guided by the same truths, encapsulated in the words of Dr. Martin Luther King, Jr.: "Injustice anywhere is a threat to justice everywhere." Sonia's story was part of what inspired me to my current work as a teacher in a public school in a seriously disadvantaged neighborhood.

At the same age as Sonia was in the forest, I organized a panel at my high school to raise awareness about the genocide in Darfur. A Sudanese refugee, then living the Bay Area, came to bear witness. Mr. Ibrahim spoke of his village and how he was among a handful of survivors out of 200 friends and family members. In a voice shaking with despair, frustration, and urgency, he begged us to do something. Watching the tears stream down his face, I felt an intense connection to this man, as if his family and mine had the same story. That was the moment I realized that human suffering cannot be compared—it is simply shared.

We live in a world where injustice and bigotry, persecution and genocide, have still not been conquered. Sometimes this feels overwhelming. But I know I will always find strength and inspiration to keep doing my small part, when I think of my grandmother—the strongest woman I know.

EVA ORBUCH (23)
San Jose, California

A POEM, INSPIRED BY A GRANDFATHER

I wrote this poem as a teenager, more than forty years ago, about my grandfather, Wolf Shainwald, who led his wife and daughter—my mother, Sonia—out of the Luboml Ghetto in Poland and into the forest in a desperate quest for survival during the Holocaust. Their story is recounted, above, by my daughter, Eva.

Wolf and Sonia made their way from behind the Iron Curtain to a Displaced Persons camp in American-occupied Germany. (His wife—my grandmother—succumbed to typhus shortly after the war.) They emigrated to the U.S. in 1948. He, with his second wife, Chava (whom I fully viewed and loved as my grandmother), always lived with us in our two-family house in New York; I saw him every day after school. He was a gentle soul.

More than a decade ago, inspired by their little-known acts of resistance, I became the founding President of the Jewish Partisan Educational

Foundation, www.jewishpartisans.org, which provides state-of-the-art educational tools and curricula to more than 7,000 educators worldwide, in the hope that they and their students will stand up early against injustice wherever it occurs.

"Let the Children Know"

Dead men
Traced in your worn face,
Grandfather.
An old man smiling easily.

I creep upstairs into your lap
To join a "Chapters of The Fathers,
To watch the sunset
Together.

Mother tells of the year
Crawling in the forest (after *Judenrein*)
Trading watches for potatoes,
Waiting in a barn
For the Gestapo
You shot between the eyes.

Your home,
All things familiar
Burned by a German fist.
Your daughter, hollow-eyed,
Instantly a woman.

You sit at peace now,
In sunsets,
Quoting from the Fathers,
Teach me to bind my arms
In the leather straps,
You say: We survive by strapping Jew to Jew
anchored to a stone wall in Zion.

I know better,
You survived by killing.
An Ancient scene.
You are at peace for having killed.
Let the children know, Grandfather.

**PAUL ORBUCH
(Wolf's grandson/Sonia's
son/Eva's father)
San Anselmo, California**

Readers:

This final letter (below) isn't from a grandchild. It is about one. I was very moved by Esther Manewith's story, originally published in the Chicago Tribune on April 15, 2010. Young Nate is doing beautifully, and he and his mother have since moved to Chicago to be near family.

—Jerry Witkovsky

A RUSSIAN ADOPTION

The enormity of what we had done didn't hit me until we were saying our goodbyes at Dulles International Airport in D.C.

My husband Bob and I had just returned with our daughter, Toby, from three weeks in Russia where she had completed a foreign adoption. Igor Sergeivitch Kaleznik, age just-turned-two, was now hers. And ours.

"Please," I asked one more time, "let Dad and I come home with you for a few days."

"No," she replied, "I have to bond with him on my own."

"So, you bond, I'll do the laundry."

"No," she said with the familiar determined set to her lips that I knew so well. "I have to do this by myself."

So we hugged and kissed, and Toby, a single parent, put Igor in his stroller and left for her own apartment. We got into the security line for the flight back to Chicago. I cried.

It wasn't going to be easy. Igor bit when he wasn't happy. He hit and scratched when he couldn't have something he wanted. He threw food on the floor and toys in the toilet. He had the ability to take off his pants and diaper and urinate on the floor. He pulled off our glasses (we all wear glasses) when he didn't know how to handle a situation.

He had spent all of his two years at Orphanage No. 4 in Rostov, Russia, (one of 40 orphanages in the province) where the director told us, "You must always say 'no' to him; we raise our children to be tough because it's a tough world out there and they must be tough to cope with it."

And tough they were. On the orphanage playground, where the ages ranged from 18 months to four years, the children bit and scratched each other over toys and turns on the see-saw. They fought over where to sit and where to stand. The caregivers, all peasant women, intervened only when things got really rough. Generally, they let the children work things out themselves—even the littlest ones just starting to walk had to learn to defend themselves.

Today, almost nine months later, Igor—now Nathaniel Benjamin and called "Nate"—is a darling and delightful child. He is in nursery school two mornings a week and plays well with others. He loves the park and playground. He no longer throws food on the floor or items into the toilet. He speaks English now and can say "I'm mad!" instead of biting or hitting.

How did all this come about? Through months and months of patience and endless loving care from our daughter. Through limitless hours and hours of playing, singing and dancing with him. Through infinite readings of books and playing in the sink with water toys. Through time spent with therapists, social workers and nursery school directors. Through months and weeks and days spent devoted to Nate. Through rough-housing and tumbling around and carrying him on her shoulders. Through making pizza together. And, when the snow blanketed Washington this winter, through unbelievable hours spent together marching up and down the hallways of the apartment building singing.

In one way, Toby was fortunate. Her profession as a rabbi allows her to office at home and spend more valuable hours with her son. When she is at the synagogue on Friday night and Saturday morning, or when she teaches a class or meets with congregants or with the board of directors, she has a couple of super baby sitters whom Nate has come to adore.

He is the love of her life. As most mothers, she knew she would love her child, but never realized how absolutely crazy she would be about him. Everything he does, everything he says, she reports to us on the phone when we speak daily.

We have been to D.C. several times and plan to go again, for his third birthday, in July.

Friends keep saying what a lucky little boy he is to have found a loving family. No, we are the lucky ones. To Bob and me, he is a gift, a blessing, a special child. To Toby, he is everything and the soul that completes her life.

ESTHER L. MANEWITH
Chicago, Illinois

Journaling Expedition #10:

Endnotes

Here's a place to aggregate your own list of grandparenting resources (books, web links, organizations, experts) in the areas that speak to your needs and interests.

_____

_____

_____

_____

_____

_____

GRAND THOUGHTS

"The best babysitters, of course, are the baby's grandparents. You feel completely comfortable entrusting your baby to them for long periods, which is why most grandparents flee to Florida."
—Dave Barry

"The presence of a grandparent confirms that parents were, indeed, little once too, and that people who are little can grow to be big, can become parents, and one day even have grandchildren of their own. So often we think of grandparents as belonging to the past; but in this important way, grandparents, for young children, belong to the future."
—Fred Rogers

"What is it about grandparents that is so lovely? I'd like to say that grandparents are God's gifts to children. And if they can but see, hear and feel what these people have to give, they can mature at a fast rate."
—Bill Cosby

"What children need most are the essentials that grandparents provide in abundance. They give unconditional love, kindness, patience, humor, comfort, lessons in life. And, most importantly, cookies."
—Rudolph Giuliani

"A house needs a grandma in it."
—Louisa May Alcott

"Only the family, society's smallest unit, can change and yet maintain enough continuity to rear children who will not be 'strangers in a strange land,' who will be rooted firmly enough to grow and adapt."
—Salvador Minuchin, MD (*Families and Family Therapy*)

"My grandmother started walking five miles a day when she was 60. She's 97 now, and we don't know where the heck she is."
—Ellen DeGeneres

"After a good dinner one can forgive anybody, even one's own relatives."
—Oscar Wilde

"And then it occurs to me. They are frightened. In me, they see their own daughters, just as ignorant, just as unmindful of all the truths and hopes they have brought to America. They see daughters who grow impatient when their mothers talk in Chinese, who think they are stupid when they explain things in fractured English. They see that joy and luck do not mean the same to their daughters, that to these closed American-born minds "joy luck" is not a word, it does not exist. They see daughters who will bear grandchildren born without any connecting hope passed from generation to generation."
—Amy Tan (*The Joy Luck Club*)

"Show me a family of readers, and I will show you the people who move the world."
—Napoleon Bonaparte

"Maybe children just want whatever it is they don't get. And then they grow up and give their children what they wanted, be it silence or information, affection or independence—so that child, in turn, craves something else. With every generation the pendulum swings from opposite to opposite, stillness and peace so elusive."
—Laura Moriarty (*The Rest of Her Life*)

"Learning is ever young, even in old age."

—Aeschylus

"We should all have one person who knows how to bless us despite the evidence. Grandmother was that person to me."

—Phyllis Theroux

"The goal of forgiveness is not to erase the past, but rather to embrace it in a way that transforms all the persons involved into healthier and more productive individuals."

—Michael T.
Witkovsky, MD

"Nobody can do for little children what grandparents do. Grandparents sort of sprinkle stardust over the lives of little children."

—Alex Haley

"A grandmother pretends she doesn't know who you are on Halloween."

—Erma Bombeck

"She [grandmother] seems to have had the ability to stand firmly on the rock of her past while living completely and unregretfully in the present."

—Madeleine L'Engle

"Our attitudes toward retirement, marriage, recreation, even our feelings about death and dying, may make much more of an impression than we realize."

—Eda J. LeShan

"No two people—no mere father and mother—as I have often said, are enough to provide emotional security for a child. He needs to feel himself one in a world of kinfolk, persons of variety in age and temperament, and yet allied to himself by an indissoluble bond which he cannot break if he could, for nature has welded him into it before he was born."

—Pearl S. Buck

"Elephants and grandchildren never forget."

—Andy Rooney

"I loved their home. Everything smelled older, worn but safe; the food aroma had baked itself into the furniture."

—Susan Strasberg

"No one fights dirtier or more brutally than blood; only family knows it's own weaknesses, the exact placement of the heart. The tragedy is that one can still live with the force of hatred, feel infuriated that once you are born to another, that kinship lasts through life and death, immutable, unchanging, no matter how great the misdeed or betrayal. Blood cannot be denied, and perhaps that's why we fight tooth and claw, because we cannot—being only human—put asunder what God has joined together."

—Whitney Otto (How to Make an American Quilt)

"It never takes longer than a few minutes, when they get together, for everyone to revert to the state of nature, like a party marooned by a shipwreck. That's what a family is. Also the storm at sea, the ship, and the unknown shore. And the hats and the whiskey stills that you make out of bamboo and coconuts. And the fire that you light to keep away the beasts."

—Michael Chabon (The Yiddish Policemen's Union)

"To forget one's ancestors is to be a brook without a source, a tree without a root."

—Chinese proverb

ACKNOWLEDGMENTS

The Grandest Love was principally guided by three women. Organizational development professional Pearl Lerner Kane, my cherished lifelong friend, steadfastly believed in this project and in my ideas of family. I thank her for putting together the talented team that made this book a reality. Vivien Orbach-Smith, my discerning editor, was the passionate heart, tenacious spirit, and creative soul who took my book from an academic-sounding treatise to one that portrays the deep humanity and universality of family relationships. And Susan Sanders Witkow's dedication, incisiveness, and attention to detail were truly invaluable. I thank her for her expert production coordination and research, and for sharing her own delightful grandparenting adventure.

I am greatly indebted to Dr. Joan Maltese for graciously agreeing to write the Foreword. It was hugely gratifying to receive such an eloquent endorsement from this esteemed child-development expert and to learn that my ideas will be shared with a new generation of helping professionals committed to children and families. I am grateful too to the distinguished individuals from a variety of vocations, who graciously provided advance praise: Patricia Heath, Dr. Felice Kaufmann, Judi Luepke, Maxine Paul, Rabbi Joel H. Meyers, and Bruce L. Mondschain. Thank you also to Jenna Rosen for cutting away the weeds and thistles from my early writing.

My heartfelt thanks to all those who generously contributed extraordinarily affecting personal stories to be included in *The*

Grandest Love. Their memorable experiences and insights, across generations and a wide array of cultures, beautifully illuminate my book's central message: that grandparents can have a profound impact and an enduring legacy.

The greatest treasures of a long and full life are the fine people you connect with along the way. Bruce Mondschain is not only a good friend and associate; he and his wife, Ellen, are grandparents with a marvelous gift for family living with meaning and creativity. And for their loving friendship and support, I am forever grateful to Felice Padnos, Lois Rosen, Cynthia Hirsch, Nort Wasserman, Ernie Kaufman, Mike Palatnik, Kevin Quigley of Kevin's Restaurant, and my wonderful Aunt Shirley Silverman.

Through the decades, my professional life and personal outlook were immeasurably enriched by many, many distinguished associates at the Jewish Community Centers of Chicago and at Camp CHI—administration, staff, and board members alike. Special thanks to Elaine Frank, Laurie Lieberman, Chuck Frank, Bob Katz, Abe Vinik, Ron Levin, Harlan Haimes, Richard Nelson, Perry Snyderman, and the legendary Mr. and Mrs. Chi Winkle. I have been inspired, too, by the important work of Sharon Morton, founder of Grandparents for Social Action.

One of my most rewarding undertakings, in recent years, has been to spearhead orientation programs for grandparents of students attending Chicago-area high schools, to help the generations remain connected through those important years. I am immensely gratified by the growing number of institutions that are incorporating this exciting program into their curricula. I particularly wish to acknowledge those at the "pilot" school, Deerfield High: principal Audris Griffith; science department chair Judi Luepke, my faculty liaison; and the enthusiastic students who produce the "Grand Connection" newsletter for the school website.

Finally, I am forever grateful to my family. Their challenging inquiries, wise input, and ongoing support have made this book possible; our love for one another makes *all* things possible. Love is the engine that propels three generations to keep on Teaching and Learning and to thrive independently and interdependently. This is a joy and a blessing I never take for granted.

JERRY WITKOVSKY
Deerfield, Illinois
June 2013

"THE GRANDCHILDREN SPEAK"
INDEX OF CONTRIBUTORS

B

Backer, Martha Kapler, 170
Beser, Erin, 200
Bhatt, Foram, 25
Bronson, Spencer R., 217
Burstein, Irene, 165

C

Cervantes, Jessica Anne, 201–3
Cervantes, Kathryn, 193, 196
Charalambides, Ana, 72
Citrin, Michelle, 129, 131
Cohen, Alex, 216
Cornfield, Marc, 73

E

Eisen, G. S., 189–90

F

Fanwick, Emily, 70
Filipovic, Jill, 88–89

G

Gibney, Christy, 215–16

H

Howard, Barbara, 162–63

K

Kane, Molly G., 108, 110
Kaylee, 108
Khorsandi, Jessica, 134–35
Kose, Jacob, 26, 28
Kress, Jeremy, 150

M

Manewith, Esther L., 131–34,
   221–23
Mclaughlin, Denise, 167, 170
McMillen, Patricia R., 73
Mendelson Graf, Alysa, 70–71

N

Negrin, Daniel, 166

O

Orbach, Rachel Claire, 171
Orbach-Smith, Vivien, 89, 91, 229
Orbuch, Eva, 217, 219
Orbuch, Paul, 219, 221
O. S., Arielle, 151–52

Q

Quigley, Coleen, 163–64

R

R., Keren, 215
Rabbits, Jesse J., 26
Robin, 172
Rosenbaum, Avi, 151

S

S., Jordan, 167
Scheinthal, Ari, 187–88
Schnoll, Noah, 167
Silverman, Stephen M., 91
Sinha, Adya, 48–50
Steiner, Nancy Sokoler, 47

T

T., Jack, 189
Tanzer, Myles, 47
Tartakovsky, Joseph Friedman, 108

V

Vij, Priya, 163

W

Williams, Anna J., 48
Witkovsky, Aidan, 194
Witkovsky, Benny, 193, 195
Witkovsky, Ethan, 198, 200
Witkovsky, Merete, 194
Witkow, Sanders, 26
Witkow, Stanley, 140, 167

Z

Z.H., 134
Zorek-Pressman, Jennifer, 70

ABOUT THE AUTHOR

JERRY WITKOVSKY (MSW, University of Illinois) is a beloved mentor to thousands of individuals and generations of families, thanks to 47 years of professional leadership—18 of them as general director—of the Jewish Community Centers of Chicago. In 1995, he was named one of the city's "Most Effective Nonprofit CEOs" by Crain's *Chicago Business Magazine*. Since his 1997 retirement, Jerry has focused his considerable energies on grandparenting facilitation, helping multigenerational families work (and play) together to create a rich family life. He currently spearheads a growing number of school-based programs designed to strengthen connections between grandparents and their teenaged grandchildren.

More Advance Praise for *The Grandest Love:*

"Jerry Witkovsky has been a role model, lecturer, program-developer and tireless advocate for **the unique role that grandparents play in the three-generation interplay.** His vision has served as the blueprint for grandparenting initiatives under the rubric of Catalyst Benefits' 250+ hospital-based, aging-adult membership programs. With imagination and energy, he captures the passion that grandparents feel for their grandchildren, creates opportunities for them to be active participants in each other's lives, and helps them deal with the challenges they may face. An important and inviting compilation of Jerry's well-honed philosophy, with wonderful stories from grandchildren that will warm the heart and soul of the reader."
BRUCE L. MONDSCHAIN, President, Catalyst Associates, Inc.

"The author guides us along a path that will leave a lasting legacy for our grandchildren, while strengthening our bonds with our adult children. As it was written in the biblical Book of Proverbs: **'Grandchildren are the crown of their elders, and the glory of children is their parents (17:6).'** *The Grandest Love* helps make this a reality for us all."
RABBI JOEL H. MEYERS, Executive VP Emeritus, The Rabbinical Assembly

"Jerry initiated a marvelous program at our school that helps grandparents **connect with their teenaged grandchildren during these crucial years of their development.** Just as new moms and dads seek out books on parenting, new grandparents should read this one to guide them in their important role."
JUDI LUEPKE, Science Dept. Chair, Deerfield (IL) High School

"The Grandest Love challenges us **to 'Teach-and-Learn' organically and to** revel in our own unique stories. Jerry's thought-provoking **Journaling Expeditions are excellent vehicles for self-knowledge.** Let his wisdom inspire your grandparenting journey, as it has mine!"
—MAXINE PAUL, Life Coach/CEO, MP Associates

CPSIA information can be obtained
at www.ICGtesting.com
Printed in the USA
FSHW011003090719
59796FS